About this book

The *German Picture Dictionary* is for everyone who is beginning to study German. Through it, you are introduced to 1,200 of the most commonly used words in both English and German.

Practically all of the words in this dictionary are illustrated with colorful, lighthearted pictures. Each illustrated word is translated and then appears in a German sentence below its picture. The sentence shows you how that word is used in German. There is also an English translation of each sentence to help you if you do not understand all of the German words.

In German, all nouns begin with a capital letter. You will notice that, in this dictionary, they all have **der, die,** or **das** (meaning "the") before them. This is because all nouns in German are masculine, feminine, or neuter (see page 82). If a noun appears in the plural form in a sentence, it is marked by an asterisk (*). Sometimes, you will see a small number above a word. This means there is a note about the word at the bottom of the page.

A German adjective changes its endings to go along with the noun it is describing (see page 83). In this dictionary, we usually show the stem of the adjective to which you add the different endings. However, with some special adjectives, the stem *and* all three basic endings are shown: **bester/e/es** (best).

When you are reading the German sentences in this dictionary, you will notice that some verbs break up into two words. You can find out more about these verbs on page 83.

There are three words for "you" in German – **du, ihr,** and **Sie. Du** and **ihr** are the words most often used among friends, so those are the words we have used.

At the back of this dictionary, there is a special section to help you learn German. You will find a pronunciation guide on page 81 and a guide to basic German grammar on pages 82-83. Numbers and useful phrases are on pages 84-85. On pages 86-95 all the words in this dictionary are listed in German alphabetical order, along with their English translation and the page where they may be located.

First published in 1986 by
National Textbook Company, 4255 West Touhy Ave., Lincolnwood, Illinois 60646-1975 U.S.A.
© 1986, 1984 National Textbook Company and Usborne Publishing Inc.

Aggie Henry Fritz Bill Ben

GERMAN
PICTURE
DICTIONARY

Angela Wilkes
Illustrated by Colin King
Translated by Sonja Osthecker

Consultant: Betty Root

Fifi   Zizi   Th ... gs   Grandpa

about   **von**

Das Buch handelt von Drachen.
The book is about dragons.

above   **über**

Der Drachen fliegt über dem Baum.
The kite is flying above the tree.

accident   **der Unfall**

Henry hat einen Unfall.
Henry has an accident.

across   **quer über**

Der Hund läuft quer über den Park.
The dog runs across the park.

actor   **der Schauspieler**[1]

Das ist ein berühmter Schauspieler.
This is a famous actor.

to add   **in . . . tun**

Aggie tut Zucker in ihren Tee.
Aggie adds sugar to her tea.

address   **die Adresse**

Hier ist Henrys Adresse.
This is Henry's address.

to be afraid   **die Angst**[2]

Der Hund hat Angst vor Mäusen.
The dog is afraid of mice.

after   **nach**

Der Dienstag kommt nach dem Montag.
Tuesday comes after Monday.

Es ist nach Mitternacht.
It is after midnight.

afternoon   **nachmittag**

Komm mich heute nachmittag besuchen.
Come and see me this afternoon.

Er spielt am Samstagnachmittag Fußball.
He plays soccer on Saturday afternoon.

again   **wieder**

Henry hat wieder einen Unfall.
Henry has an accident again.

against   **an**

Fifi lehnt sich an die Wand.
Fifi is leaning against a wall.

age   **das Alter**

Die Männer sind im gleichen Alter.
The men are the same age.

air   **die Luft**

Das Flugzeug ist in der Luft.
The airplane is in the air.

    1. actress: **die Schauspielerin.**   2. In German you say ''The dog has fear of mice.''

airplane — das Flugzeug

Dieses Flugzeug ist grün.
This airplane is green.

airport — der Flughafen

Der Pilot sieht den Flughafen.
The pilot sees the airport.

alarm clock — der Wecker

Der Wecker klingelt.
The alarm clock is ringing.

all — alle

Die Mäuse sind alle rosa.
All the mice are pink.

almost — fast

Das Puzzle ist fast fertig.
The puzzle is almost finished.

alone — allein

Fifi ist ganz allein.
Fifi is all alone.

along — entlang

Blumen wachsen am Weg entlang.
Flowers grow along the path.

alphabet — das Alphabet

All diese Buchstaben sind im Alphabet.
All these letters are in the alphabet.

already — schon

Zizi hat schon ein Törtchen.
Zizi already has a cupcake.

also — auch

Zizi ist ein Mädchen. Sie ist auch ein Baby.
Zizi is a girl. She is also a baby.

Fifi ist nicht nur schön, sie ist auch klug.
Fifi is not only beautiful, she is also smart.

always — immer

Henry hat immer Unfälle.
Henry always has accidents.

ambulance — der Krankenwagen

Der Krankenwagen kommt.
The ambulance is arriving.

among — zwischen

Die Katze versteckt sich zwischen den Vögeln.
The cat is hiding among the birds.

and — und

Hier sind Fritz und Hank.
Here are Fritz and Hank.

angel — der Engel

Der Engel fliegt durch die Luft.
The angel is flying in the sky.

angry — wütend

Der Engel ist wütend.
The angel is angry.

any — jeder/e/es

Du kannst an jedem Kiosk eine Zeitung kaufen.
You can buy a newspaper at any newsstand.

anybody — jemand

Ist hier jemand?
Is anybody there?

arm — der Arm

Ben hat sich den Arm gebrochen.
Ben has a broken arm.

animal — das Tier

Das sind alles Tiere.*
These are all animals.

apartment — die Wohnung

Fifi wohnt in einer Wohnung.
Fifi lives in an apartment.

army — die Armee

Bill ist bei der Armee.
Bill is in the army.

another — noch ein

Bill nimmt sich noch ein Törtchen.
Bill takes another cupcake.

apple — der Apfel

Fifi ißt einen Apfel.
Fifi is eating an apple.

to arrange — ordnen

Fifi ordnet die Blumen.
Fifi arranges the flowers.

answer — die Lösung[1]

Hier ist eine Rechenaufgabe und ihre Lösung.
Here is an addition problem and the answer to it.

apron — die Schürze

Bill zieht seine Schürze an.
Bill puts on his apron.

to arrive — ankommen

Der Zug kommt an.
The train is arriving.

ant — die Ameise

Die Ameise läuft über das Buch.
The ant runs over the book.

to argue — sich streiten

Bill und Ben streiten sich.
Bill and Ben are arguing.

arrow — der Pfeil

Sherlock Holmes findet einen Pfeil.
Sherlock Holmes finds an arrow.

1. The usual word for answer is **die Antwort.**

artist   **der Künstler**[1]

Der Künstler malt.
The artist is painting.

as   **als**
     so . . . wie

Es regnete, als wir fortgingen.
It was raining as we left.

Bill ist so groß wie Ben.
Bill is as tall as Ben.

to ask   **bitten**

Zizi bittet um einen Apfel.
Zizi asks for an apple.

astronaut   **der Astronaut**

Hier ist ein Astronaut.
Here is an astronaut.

at   **um**
     in
     zu

Um vier Uhr trinken wir Tee.
At four o'clock we have tea.

Fifi ist zu Hause.
Fifi is at home.

Die Kinder sind in der Schule.
The children are at school.

---

aunt   **die Tante**

Tante Aggie ist Muttis Schwester.
Aunt Aggie is Mom's sister.

(to blow) away   **wegblasen**

Der Wind bläst Bens Zeitung weg.
The wind blows Ben's newspaper away.

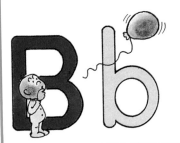

baby   **das Baby**

Das Baby weint.
The baby is crying.

baby carriage   **der Kinderwagen**

Zizi ist im Kinderwagen.
Zizi is in a baby carriage.

---

back   **der Rücken**

Henry kratzt sich den Rücken.
Henry scratches his back.

bad   **schlecht**
     schlimm

Das Wetter ist heute schlecht.
The weather is bad today.

Vater ist schlechter Laune.
Dad is in a bad mood.

Sie hat eine schlimme Erkältung.
She has a bad cold.

bag   **die Tasche**

Die Tasche ist voller Geld.
The bag is full of money.

baker   **der Bäcker**

Der Bäcker bäckt Brot.
The baker makes bread.

ball   **der Ball**

Max fängt den Ball.
Max catches the ball.

---

1. A lady artist: **die Künstlerin.**

7

| balloon | **der Ballon** | to bark | **bellen** | beach | **der Strand** |

Zizi läuft hinter dem Ballon her.
Zizi chases the balloon.

Der Hund bellt.
The dog is barking.

Fifi liegt am Strand.
Fifi is lying on the beach.

| banana | **die Banane** | baseball | **der Baseball** | beak | **der Schnabel** |

Ein großes Bündel Bananen.*
A big bunch of bananas.

Henry spielt Baseball.
Henry is playing baseball.

Der Vogel hat einen roten Schnabel.
The bird has a red beak.

| band | **die Kapelle** | basket | **der Korb** | bean | **die Bohne** |

Die Kapelle spielt.
The band is playing.

Der Korb ist voll Äpfel.
The basket is full of apples.

Das sind grüne Bohnen.*
These are green beans.

| bank | **das Ufer** | bathroom | **das Bade-zimmer** | bear | **der Bär** |

Jim liegt am Flußufer.
Jim is on the river bank.

Die Badewanne ist im Badezimmer.
The bathtub is in the bathroom.

Bruno ist ein brauner Bär.
Bruno is a brown bear.

| bank | **die Bank** | bathtub | **die Badewanne** | beard | **der Bart** |

Fred rennt aus der Bank weg.
Fred runs away from the bank.

Die Katze ist in der Badewanne.
The cat is in the bathtub.

Der Mann hat einen langen Bart.
The man has a long beard.

| beautiful | schön | beef | das Rindfleisch | bell | die Glocke |

Eine schöne Prinzessin.
A beautiful princess.

Bob schneidet das Rindfleisch.
Bob is slicing the beef.

Die Glocke läutet.
The bell is ringing.

| because | weil | before | vor, vorher | bellboy | der Gepäckträger |

Das Baby schreit, weil es Hunger hat.
The baby is crying because she is hungry.

Er ist dick, weil er zuviel ißt.
He is fat because he eats too much.

Der Montag kommt vor dem Dienstag.
Monday comes before Tuesday.

Es ist vor Mitternacht.
It is before midnight.

Warum hast du mir das nicht vorher gesagt?
Why didn't you tell me before?

Ein Gepäckträger trägt Koffer.
A bellboy carries suitcases.

| bed | das Bett | to begin | anfangen | to belong | gehören |

Der König liegt im Bett.
The king is in bed.

Es fängt an zu regnen.
It is beginning to rain.

Das Spiel fängt an.
The game is beginning.

Der Film fängt um 7 Uhr an.
The movie begins at 7 o'clock.

Der Hut gehört Ben.
The hat belongs to Ben.

Wem gehört das?
Who does this belong to?

Es gehört Fifi.
It belongs to Fifi.

| bedroom | das Schlaf-zimmer | behind | hinter | below | unter |

Das Bett steht im Schlafzimmer.
The bed is in the bedroom.

Wer steht hinter dem Baum?
Who is standing behind the tree?

Die Katze sitzt zwei Stufen unter Bruno.
The cat is two stairs below Bruno.

| bee | die Biene | to believe | glauben | belt | der Gürtel |

Sam glaubt meine Geschichte.
Sam believes my story.

Sam glaubt alles, was man ihm erzählt.
Sam believes anything you tell him.

Opa glaubt an Gott.
Grandpa believes in God.

Die Biene sitzt auf einer Blume.
The bee is on a flower.

Fifi trägt einen breiten Gürtel.
Fifi is wearing a big belt.

bench **die Bank**	**bicycle** **das Fahrrad**	**black** **schwarz**

Der Vogel sitzt auf einer Bank.
The bird is sitting on a bench.

Der Bäcker fährt auf einem Fahrrad.
The baker rides on a bicycle.

Die große Katze ist schwarz.
The big cat is black.

---

to bend   **biegen**

Sam biegt einen Löffel.
Sam is bending a spoon.

big   **groß**

Der Elefant ist groß.
The elephant is big.

blackbird   **die Amsel**

Eine Amsel ist schwarz.
A blackbird is black.

---

best   **bester/e/es**

Fifi ist die beste Tänzerin.
Fifi is the best dancer.

Das ist mein bestes Kleid.
This is my best dress.

Er ist der Beste in der Klasse.
He is the best in the class.

bird   **der Vogel**

Der Vogel sitzt auf einem Fahrrad.
The bird is sitting on a bicycle.

blackboard   **die Tafel**

Ben malt an die Tafel.
Ben draws on the blackboard.

---

better   **besser**

Fifi ist eine bessere Tänzerin als Susi.
Fifi is a better dancer than Susie.

Henry spricht besser Französisch als Ben.
Henry speaks French better than Ben.

birthday   **der Geburtstag**

Heute hat Zizi Geburtstag.
Today is Zizi's birthday.

blanket   **die Decke**

Es ist eine rote Decke auf dem Bett.
There is a red blanket on the bed.

---

between   **zwischen**

Die Katze sitzt zwischen den zwei Bären.
The cat is between the two bears.

to bite   **beißen**

Der Hund beißt den Postboten.
The dog bites the mailman.

blind   **blind**

Ein Hund führt den blinden Mann.
A dog leads the blind man.

| blond | **blond** | body | **der Körper** | boot | **der Stiefel** |

Fifis Freund hat blondes Haar.
Fifi's friend has blond hair.

Sam hat einen kräftigen Körper.
Sam has a strong body.

Dieser Vogel trägt einen blauen Stiefel.
This bird is wearing a blue boot.

| blood | **das Blut** | bone | **der Knochen** | both | **beide** |

Sam hat Blut an seinem Finger.
Sam has blood on his finger.

Fluff hat einen großen Knochen.
Fluff has a big bone.

Beide Schweine sind rosa.
Both the pigs are pink.

| to blow out | **ausblasen** | bonfire | **das Feuer** | bottle | **die Flasche** |

Zizi bläst die Kerzen aus.
Zizi blows out the candles.

Das Feuer brennt.
The bonfire is burning.

Eine große Flasche Wein.
A big bottle of wine.

| blue | **blau** | book | **das Buch** | bottom | **unten** |

Das Haus ist blau.
The house is blue.

Dieses Buch handelt von Booten.
This book is about boats.

Der Frosch ist unten auf der Leiter.
The frog is at the bottom of the ladder.

| boat | **das Boot** | bookstore | **die Buchhand-lung** | bowl | **die Schale** |

Drei Männer in einem Boot.
Three men in a boat.

Bill blickt in die Buchhandlung.
Bill looks in the bookstore.

Eine Schale voll Bananen.
A bowl full of bananas.

box **die Schachtel**	**to break** **brechen**	**bridegroom** **der Bräutigam**

Die Katze schläft in einer Schachtel.
The cat sleeps in a box.

Ben bricht das Brot.
Ben breaks the bread.

... und ihr Bräutigam.
... and her bridegroom.

boy **der Junge**	**breakfast** **das Frühstück**	**bridge** **die Brücke**

Tom ist ein kleiner Junge.
Tom is a little boy.

Fifi ißt ihr Frühstück.
Fifi has her breakfast.

Bill überquert die Brücke.
Bill crosses the bridge.

bracelet **das Armband**	**to breathe** **atmen**	**bright** **hell**

Zizi trägt ein blaues Armband.
Zizi is wearing a blue bracelet.

Fische atmen unter Wasser.
Fish breathe underwater.

Der Stern leuchtet hell.
The star is bright.

branch **der Ast**	**brick** **der Ziegelstein**	**to bring** **bringen**

Der Vogel steht auf einem Ast.
The bird is standing on a branch.

Der Mann trägt einen Ziegelstein.
The man is carrying a brick.

Max bringt Bill einen Pantoffel.
Max brings Bill a slipper.

bread **das Brot**	**bride** **die Braut**	**brother** **der Bruder**

Bill schneidet das Brot.
Bill cuts the bread.

Eine schöne Braut ...
A beautiful bride ...

Bill und Ben sind Brüder.*
Bill and Ben are brothers.

brown **braun**	to build **bauen**	bump **die Unebenheit**

Bruno ist ein brauner Bär.
Bruno is a brown bear.

Der Mann baut ein Haus.
The man is building a house.

Henry fährt über eine Unebenheit.
Henry rides over a bump.

brush **die Bürste**	building **das Gebäude**	bunch **der Strauß**

Fritz reinigt seine Schuhe mit einer Bürste.
Fritz cleans his shoes with a brush.

Ein Haus ist ein Gebäude.
A house is a building.

Ein großer Strauß Blumen.
A big bunch of flowers.

bubble **die Seifenblase**	bulb **die Blumenzwiebel**	burglar **der Einbrecher**

Der Bär macht eine Seifenblase.
The bear blows a bubble.

Die Raupe sieht sich die Blumenzwiebel an.
The caterpilllar looks at the bulb.

Der Einbrecher läuft davon.
The burglar runs away.

bucket **der Eimer**	bull **der Bulle**	to burn **brennen**

Bill leert den Eimer.
Bill empties the bucket.

Der wütende Bulle jagt Bill.
The angry bull chases Bill.

Das Haus brennt.
The house is burning.

bud **die Knospe**	bulldozer **die Planierraupe**	bus **der Bus**

Die Pflanze hat eine Knospe.
The plant has one bud.

Ben fährt eine Planierraupe.
Ben drives a bulldozer.

Der Bus hält.
The bus is stopping.

13

bus stop die Bushaltestelle

Fifi wartet an der Bushaltestelle.
Fifi waits at the bus stop.

bush der Busch

Wer ist hinter dem Busch?
Who is behind the bush?

busy beschäftigt

Der Mann ist beschäftigt.
The man is busy.

but aber

Bill ißt viel, aber er ist nicht dick.
Bill eats a lot, but he is not fat.

Ich mag Süßigkeiten, aber ich mag keine Schokolade.
I like candy, but I do not like chocolate.

Ich hätte gern ein neues Kleid, aber ich habe kein Geld.
I want a new dress, but I have no money.

butcher der Metzger

Der Metzger verkauft Fleisch.
The butcher sells meat.

butter die Butter

Die Butter schmilzt.
The butter is melting.

butterfly der Schmetterling

Ein Schmetterling auf einer Blume.
A butterfly on a flower.

button das Button

Bill trägt viele Buttons.*
Bill is wearing many buttons.

to buy kaufen

Fifi kauft ein paar Bananen.
Fifi buys some bananas.

by am

Der Mann steht am Auto.
The man is by the car.

Cc

cabbage der Kohlkopf

Fifi sucht einen Kohlkopf aus.
Fifi picks out a cabbage.

café das Café

Die Freunde gehen in ein Café.
The friends go to a café.

cage der Käfig

Der Löwe ist in einem Käfig.
The lion is in a cage.

cake der Kuchen

Fifi schneidet den Kuchen.
Fifi cuts the cake.

calculator	**der Taschen-rechner**

Der Mann benutzt seinen Taschenrechner.
The man uses his calculator.

calendar	**der Kalender**

Aggie schaut auf den Kalender.
Aggie looks at the calendar.

calf	**das Kalb**

Ein Kalb mit seiner Mutter.
A calf with its mother.

to call	**rufen**

Der Bauer ruft das Kalb.
The farmer calls the calf.

camel	**das Kamel**

Henry reitet auf einem Kamel.
Henry is riding a camel.

camera	**der Fotoapparat**

Bill hat einen neuen Fotoapparat.
Bill has a new camera.

to camp	**zelten**

Bill und Ben zelten.
Bill and Ben are camping.

candle	**die Kerze**

Henry trägt eine Kerze.
Henry is carrying a candle.

candy	**die Süßigkeit**

Zizi ißt Süßigkeiten.*
Zizi is eating candy.

cap	**die Schlägermütze**

Fred trägt immer eine Schlägermütze.
Fred always wears a cap.

capital	**die Hauptstadt**

Rom ist die Hauptstadt von Italien.
Rome is the capital of Italy.

Paris ist die Hauptstadt von Frankreich.
Paris is the capital of France.

car	**der Wagen**

Fred hat einen schnellen Wagen.
Fred has a fast car.

card	**die Karte**

Sie spielen Karten.*
They are playing cards.

carpet	**der Teppich**

Der Teppich ist blau.
The carpet is blue.

carrot	**die Karotte**

Ein Bund Karotten.*
A bunch of carrots.

15

to carry	**tragen**

Zizi trägt Karotten.
Zizi is carrying carrots.

cauliflower	**der Blumenkohl**

Ein Blumenkohl in einem Korb.
A cauliflower in a basket.

chair	**der Stuhl**

Bruno sitzt auf einem Stuhl.
Bruno is sitting on a chair.

castle	**die Burg**

Die Burg liegt auf einem Hügel.
The castle is on a hill.

cave	**die Höhle**

In der Höhle ist ein Schatz.
There is a treasure in the cave.

chalk	**die Kreide**

Bruno schreibt mit Kreide.
Bruno is writing with chalk.

cat	**die Katze**

Die Katze liegt auf dem Teppich.
The cat is on the carpet.

ceiling	**die Decke**

Sam berührt die Decke.
Sam touches the ceiling.

change	**das Wechselgeld**

Bill zählt sein Wechselgeld.
Bill counts his change.

catch	**fangen**

Die Katze fängt einen Ball.
The cat is catching a ball.

cellar	**der Keller**

Der Keller ist voller Flaschen.
The cellar is full of bottles.

to change	**wechseln**

Henry wechselt ein Rad.
Henry changes a tire.

caterpillar	**die Raupe**

Die Raupe frißt ein Blatt.
The caterpillar is eating a leaf.

chain	**die Kette**

Die Uhr hängt an einer Kette.
The watch is on a chain.

to chase	**verfolgen**

Henry verfolgt einen Dieb.
Henry is chasing a thief.

cheap	billig	chest	die Brust	chimpanzee	der Schimpanse

Der Stuhl ist billig.
The chair is cheap.

Sam schlägt sich auf die Brust.
Sam is beating his chest.

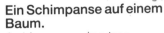

Ein Schimpanse auf einem Baum.
A chimpanzee in a tree.

---

check — **der Scheck**

chick — **das Küken**

chin — **das Kinn**

Bill schreibt einen Scheck aus.
Bill writes a check.

Die Henne hat fünf Küken.[*]
The hen has five chicks.

Sam reibt sein Kinn.
Sam rubs his chin.

---

cheek — **die Wange**

chicken — **das Hühnchen**

chocolate — **die Schokolade**

Oma hat rosa Wangen.[*]
Grandma has pink cheeks.

Ben schneidet das Hühnchen.
Ben is cutting the chicken.

Zizi ißt Schokolade.
Zizi is eating chocolate.

---

cheese — **der Käse**

child — **das Kind**

to choose — **sich aussuchen**

Fifi ißt Käse.
Fifi is eating cheese.

Die Kinder[*] **spielen.**
The children are playing.

Fifi sucht sich ein grünes Kleid aus.
Fifi chooses a green dress.

---

cherry — **die Kirsche**

chimney — **der Schornstein**

chop — **das Kotelett**

Ein Vogel frißt die Kirschen.[*]
A bird is eating the cherries.

Der Vogel sitzt auf einem Schornstein.
The bird is sitting on a chimney.

Ben ißt ein Kotelett zum Abendessen.
Ben has a pork chop for dinner.

Christmas	Weihnachten	class	die Klasse	cliff	die Klippe

Es ist Weihnachten.
It is Christmas.

In der Klasse sind fünf Kinder.
There are five children in the class.

Henry steht auf einer Klippe.
Henry is on a cliff.

church	die Kirche	classroom	das Klassen-zimmer	to climb	klettern

Fifi geht zur Kirche.
Fifi goes to church.

Das Klassenzimmer ist leer.
The classroom is empty.

Sam klettert auf eine Klippe.
Sam is climbing up the cliff.

circle	der Kreis	clean	sauber	clock	die Uhr

  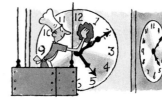

Die Küken laufen im Kreis herum.
The chicks are running in a circle.

Bill bindet sich eine saubere Schürze um.
Bill puts on a clean apron.

Ben macht die Uhr sauber.
Ben is cleaning the clock.

circus	der Zirkus	to clean	sauber machen	to close	schließen

Ein Clown im Zirkus.
A clown at the circus.

Henry macht sein Auto sauber.
Henry is cleaning his car.

Fifi schließt das Fenster.
Fifi closes the window.

city	die Großstadt	clever	klug	closet	der Schrank

New York ist eine Großstadt.
New York is a city.

Ein kluger Mensch lernt schnell.
A clever man learns fast.

Fifi blickt in den Schrank.
Fifi looks in the closet.

| cloud | **die Wolke** | coffee | **der Kaffee** | to comb | **kämmen** |

Der Engel liegt auf einer Wolke.
The angel is on a cloud.

Fifi gießt den Kaffee ein.
Fifi pours the coffee.

Fifi kämmt ihr Haar.
Fifi combs her hair.

| clown | **der Clown** | coin | **die Münze** | to come | **kommen** |

Ein Clown aus dem Zirkus.
A clown from the circus.

Fifi steckt Münzen* in ihre Tasche.
Fifi puts coins in her purse.

Die Ente kommt zu Zizi.
The duck comes to Zizi.

| coast | **die Küste** | cold | **kalt** | comforter | **das Federbett** |

Bäume wachsen an der Küste entlang.
Trees grow along the coast.

Oscar ist es kalt.
Oscar is cold.

Fifi hat ein rosa Federbett.
Fifi has a pink comforter.

| coat | **der Mantel** | color | **die Farbe** | comic book | **das Comic** |

Der Mantel des Königs ist zu groß.
The king's coat is too big.

Wieviele Farben* kannst du sehen?
How many colors can you see?

Die Jungen lesen ein Comic.
The boys are reading a comic book.

| cobweb | **das Spinnen-gewebe** | comb | **der Kamm** | computer | **der Computer** |

Eine Spinne macht ein Spinnengewebe.
A spider makes a cobweb.

Fifi hat einen großen Kamm.
Fifi has a big comb.

Brains arbeitet an einem Computer.
Brains works on a computer.

conductor **der Dirigent**	to cough **husten**	cow **die Kuh**

Herbert ist Dirigent.
Herbert is a conductor.

Fifi hustet.
Fifi is coughing.

Ein Huhn sitzt auf der Kuh.
A hen is sitting on the cow.

to cook **kochen**	to count **zählen**	cowboy **der Cowboy**

Henry kocht das Essen.
Henry is cooking dinner.

Zizi zählt die Törtchen.
Zizi is counting the cupcakes.

Ein Cowboy verfolgt eine Kuh.
A cowboy chases a cow.

cork **der Korken**	country **das Land**	crab **der Krebs**

Der Korken fliegt heraus.
The cork pops out.

England ist ein kleines Land.
England is a small country.

China und Indien sind große Länder. *
China and India are big countries.

Der Krebs läuft seitwärts.
The crab runs sideways.

corner **die Ecke**	country **das Land**	crane **der Kran**

Ruff sitzt in der Ecke.
Ruff is in a corner.

Dan wohnt auf dem Land.
Dan lives in the country.

Der Kran hebt den Wagen.
The crane is lifting the car.

to cost **kosten**	to cover **bedecken**	crayon **der Farbstift**

Der Ring kostet 1000 Mark.
The ring costs 1000 Marks.

Bill bedeckt seinen Kopf.
Bill covers his head.

Zizi malt mit Farbstiften. *
Zizi draws with crayons.

20

cream **die Sahne**	to cry **weinen**	curtain **der Vorhang**

Auf dem Kuchen ist Sahne.
There is cream on the cake.

Der König weint.
The king is crying.

Fifi macht die Vorhänge* auf.
Fifi opens the curtains.

crocodile **das Krokodil**	cube **der Würfel**	cushion **das Kissen**

Das Krokodil schläft.
The crocodile is asleep.

Ein Würfel hat sechs Seiten.
A cube has six sides.

Die Krone liegt auf einem Kissen.
The crown is on a cushion.

cross **das Kreuz**	cucumber **die Gurke**	customer **der Kunde**

Zwei Mäuse auf einem roten Kreuz.
Two mice on a red cross.

Die Gurke ist grün.
The cucumber is green.

Ein Kunde kauft Brot.
A customer buys bread.

to cross **überqueren**	cup **die Tasse**	to cut **schneiden**

Henry überquert die Straße.
Henry is crossing the street.

Eine Raupe schaut in eine Tasse.
A caterpillar looks into a cup.

Fifi schneidet Ben die Haare.
Fifi is cutting Ben's hair.

crown **die Krone**	cupboard **der Küchen-schrank**	to cut out **ausschneiden**

Der König trägt eine Krone.
The king wears a crown.

Die Tasse ist im Küchenschrank.
The cup is in the cupboard.

Sie schneidet ein Bild aus.
She cuts out a picture.

Dd

to dance — tanzen

Fifi tanzt mit Sam.
Fifi is dancing with Sam.

dancer — die Tänzerin[1]

Sie möchte Tänzerin werden.
She wants to be a dancer.

danger — die Gefahr

Henry ist in Gefahr.
Henry is in danger.

to dare — sich trauen

Er traut sich nicht hinunterzuspringen.
He does not dare to dive.

dark — dunkel

Das Zimmer ist dunkel.
The room is dark.

daughter — die Tochter

Zizi ist Marys Tochter.
Zizi is Mary's daughter.

day — der Tag

Ein Jahr hat 365 Tage. *
There are 365 days in a year.

Eine Woche hat sieben Tage. *
There are seven days in a week.

dead — tot

Max stellt sich tot.
Max pretends to be dead.

to decide — sich entschließen

Bill entschließt sich, ein Auto zu kaufen.
Bill decides to buy a car.

Entschließ dich, welches Kleid du möchtest.
Decide which dress you want.

deep — tief

Fifi ist im tiefen Wasser.
Fifi is in deep water.

deer — der Hirsch

Ein Hirsch trifft Max.
A deer meets Max.

dentist — der Zahnarzt

Henry geht zum Zahnarzt.
Henry visits the dentist.

to describe — beschreiben

Bill beschreibt der Polizei den Dieb.
Bill describes the thief to the police.

Kannst du das Bild beschreiben?
Can you describe the picture?

desert — die Wüste

Kamele leben in der Wüste.
Camels live in the desert.

1. male dancer: **der Tänzer.**

desk	**der Schreibtisch**	to dig	**graben**	dirty	**schmutzig**

Jake arbeitet an seinem Schreibtisch.
Jake works at his desk.

Max gräbt ein Loch.
Max is digging a hole.

Der Dinosaurier ist schmutzig.
The dinosaur is dirty.

diamond	**der Diamant**	dining room	**das Eßzimmer**	dish	**die Schüssel**

Fred findet einen Diamanten.
Fred finds a diamond.

Die Mäuse essen im Eßzimmer.
The mice eat in the dining room.

Eine Schüssel voll Erdbeeren.
A dish full of strawberries.

dictionary	**das Wörterbuch**	dinner	**das Essen**	to do	**tun**

Fritz hat ein Wörterbuch.
Fritz has a dictionary.

Das Ungeheuer ißt sein Essen.
The monster is eating his dinner.

Henry tut nichts.
Henry is not doing anything.

to die	**sterben**	dinosaur	**der Dinosaurier**	doctor	**die Ärztin**[1]

Henrys Pflanze stirbt.
Henry's plant is dying.

Ein Dinosaurier beim Essen.
A dinosaur eating his dinner.

Die Ärztin untersucht Sam.
The doctor examines Sam.

different	**verschieden**	direction	**die Richtung**	dog	**der Hund**

Männer mit verschiedenen Hüten.
Men in different hats.

Max dreht sich in die andere Richtung.
Max changes direction.

Der Hund läuft hinter einem Kaninchen her.
The dog is chasing a rabbit.

1. male doctor: **der Arzt.**

doghouse **die Hundehütte**	dragon **der Drachen**	to dress **anziehen**

Ruff schläft in einer Hundehütte.
Ruff sleeps in a doghouse.

Der Drachen speit Feuer.
The dragon breathes fire.

Fifi zieht Zizi an.
Fifi is dressing Zizi.

doll **die Puppe**	to draw **zeichnen**	to drink **trinken**

Zizi spielt mit einer Puppe.
Zizi is playing with a doll.

Fifi zeichnet einen Drachen.
Fifi is drawing a dragon.

Sam trinkt Milch.
Sam is drinking milk.

donkey **der Esel**	drawing **die Zeichnung**	to drive **fahren**

Henry reitet auf einem Esel.
Henry is riding a donkey.

Hier ist ihre Zeichnung.
This is her drawing.

Henry fährt mit seinem Auto.
Henry is driving his car.

door **die Tür**	to dream **träumen**	to drop **fallenlassen**

Fifi schließt die Tür.
Fifi shuts the door.

Henry träumt von Spinnen.
Henry dreams about spiders.

Henry läßt ein Ei fallen.
Henry drops an egg.

downstairs **unten**	dress **das Kleid**	drugstore **die Apotheke**

Die Puppe ist unten.
The doll is downstairs.

Fifi trägt ein langes Kleid.
Fifi is wearing a long dress.

Henry ist in der Apotheke.
Henry is at the drugstore.

| drum | **die Trommel** | each | **jeder/e/es** | east | **der Osten** |

Fred spielt auf seiner Trommel.
Fred is playing his drum.

Jedes Kind hat ein Törtchen.
Each child has a cupcake.

Der Vogel blickt nach Osten.
The bird is facing east.

| dry | **trocken** | eagle | **der Adler** | Easter | **das Ostern** |

Der Boden ist sehr trocken.
The ground is very dry.

Der Adler sitzt auf seinem Nest.
The eagle is in its nest.

Ostern ist ein kirchliches Fest im Frühjahr.
Easter is a religious holiday in the spring.

Am Ostersonntag gehen viele Leute zur Kirche.
Many people go to church on Easter Sunday.

| duck | **die Ente** | ear | **das Ohr** | easy | **leicht** |

Die Ente schwimmt in der Badewanne.
The duck is in the bathtub.

Der Esel hat lange Ohren. *
The donkey has long ears.

Der Kuchen ist leicht zu backen.
The cake is easy to make.

Sams Hausaufgaben sind leicht.
Sam's homework is easy.

| dust | **der Staub** | early | **früh** | easy chair | **der Sessel** |

Max wälzt sich im Staub.
Max rolls in the dust.

Ben steht früh am Morgen auf.
Ben gets up early in the morning.

Ich komme früh nach Hause.
I am coming home early.

Die Katze liegt auf dem Sessel.
The cat is lying on the easy chair.

| earth | **die Erde** | to eat | **essen**[1] |

Die Erde ist rund.
The earth is round.

Zizi ißt Schokolade.
Zizi is eating chocolate.

---

1. In German there are two words for "to eat." **Essen** for people and **fressen** for animals.

| edge   **die Kante** | empty   **leer** | entrance   **der Eingang** |

edge   **die Kante**

Zizi sitzt auf der Tischkante.
Zizi is on the edge of the table.

empty   **leer**

Die Tasche ist leer.
The bag is empty.

entrance   **der Eingang**

Der Eingang zu einer Höhle.
The entrance to a cave.

egg   **das Ei**

Zizi ißt ein Ei.
Zizi is eating an egg.

to empty   **leeren**

Henry leert den Eimer.
Henry empties the bucket.

envelope   **der Umschlag**

Fifi öffnet den Umschlag.
Fifi opens the envelope.

elbow   **der Ellbogen**

Henry stößt sich den Ellbogen.
Henry hits his elbow.

end   **das Ende**

Die Maus hängt am Ende des Seils.
The mouse is hanging at the end of the rope.

to escape   **entkommen**

Der Sträfling entkommt.
The prisoner escapes.

elephant   **der Elefant**

Ein Elefant hat große Ohren.
An elephant has big ears.

enough   **genug**

Fifi hat genug Geld, um sich ein neues Auto zu kaufen.
Fifi has enough money to buy a new car.

Hast du genug zu essen?
Do you have enough to eat?

evening   **der Abend**

Abends geht die Sonne unter.
The sun sets in the evening.

elevator   **der Lift**

Henry steigt in den Lift.
Henry enters the elevator.

to enter   **betreten**

Der König betritt das Zimmer.
The king enters the room.

every   **jeder/e/es**

Jedes Schwein ist rosa.
Every pig is pink.

everyone	**alle**

Alle tragen einen Hut.
Everyone is wearing a hat.

everything	**alles**

Alles ist grün.
Everything is green.

everywhere	**überall**

Fifi sucht überall nach ihrer Katze.
Fifi looks everywhere for her cat.

Mein Hund läuft mir überallhin nach.
My dog follows me everywhere.

except	**außer**

Alle Schweine außer einem sind rosa.
Every pig is pink except one.

exciting	**aufregend**

Jake liest ein aufregendes Buch.
Jake reads an exciting book.

experiment	**das Experi-ment**

Brains macht ein Experiment.
Brains does an experiment.

to explain	**erklären**

Fifi erklärt, warum sie ein Auto haben möchte.
Fifi explains why she wants a car.

Erklär mir, wie das geht.
Explain to me how this works.

eye	**das Auge**

Die Katze hat blaue Augen.*
The cat has blue eyes.

face	**das Gesicht**

Fifi wäscht sich das Gesicht.
Fifi is washing her face.

factory	**die Fabrik**

Der Mann arbeitet in einer Fabrik.
The man works in a factory.

fairy	**die Elfe**

Die Elfe sitzt auf einer Blume.
The fairy sits on a flower.

to fall	**fallen**

Die Elfe fällt herunter.
The fairy falls off.

family	**die Familie**

Fifis Familie.
Fifi's family.

famous	**berühmt**

Will ist ein berühmter Künstler.
Will is a famous artist.

far	**weit**	father	**der Vater**	feet[1]	**die Füße***

Das Haus ist weit weg.
The house is far away.

Zizi ist bei ihrem Vater.
Zizi is with her father.

Hier sind zwei große Füße.*
Here are two big feet.

farm	**der Bauernhof**	faucet	**der Wasserhahn**	fence	**der Zaun**

Der Bauernhof liegt auf dem Land.
The farm is in the country.

Die Maus dreht den Wasserhahn auf.
The mouse turns on the faucet.

Die Kuh springt über den Zaun.
The cow jumps over the fence.

farmer	**der Bauer**	feather	**die Feder**	few	**wenig**

Der Bauer lebt auf einem Bauernhof.
The farmer lives on a farm.

Ein Vogel mit gelben Federn.*
A bird with yellow feathers.

Dieser Vogel hat wenige Federn.
This bird has few feathers.

fast	**schnell**	to feed	**füttern**	field	**die Weide**

Der Bauer läuft schnell.
The farmer runs fast.

Zizi füttert die Enten.
Zizi is feeding the ducks.

Die Kühe sind auf der Weide.
The cows are in the field.

fat	**dick**	to feel	**fühlen**	to fight	**sich schlagen**

Diese Elfe ist dick.
This fairy is fat.

Bill kann den Stuhl fühlen.
Bill feels the chair.

Bill und Ben schlagen sich.
Bill and Ben are fighting.

to fill **füllen**	firemen[1] **die Feuerwehr-männer***	to fix **reparieren**

Fifi füllt das Glas.
Fifi fills the glass.

Die Feuerwehrmänner* löschen das Feuer.
The firemen put out the fire.

Ben repariert sein Fahrrad.
Ben is fixing his bicycle.

to find **finden**	fireworks **das Feuerwerk**[2]	flag **die Fahne**

Bill findet sein Buch.
Bill finds his book.

Ein Feuerwerk am Himmel.
Fireworks in the sky.

Henry trägt eine Fahne.
Henry is carrying a flag.

finger **der Finger**	first **erster/e/es**	flame **die Flamme**

Vier Finger* und ein Daumen.
Four fingers and a thumb.

Bill ist der erste in der Schlange.
Bill is first in line.

Zizi bläst die Flamme aus.
Zizi blows out the flame.

finished **fertig**	fish **der Fisch**	flat **flach**

Fifi ist mit ihrem Essen fertig.
Fifi has finished her dinner.

Ein großer Fisch und ein kleiner Fisch.
A big fish and a little fish.

Dieses Haus hat ein flaches Dach.
This house has a flat roof.

fire **das Feuer**	to fish **angeln**	floor **der Boden**

Die Männer sitzen am Feuer.
The men sit by the fire.

Johann angelt.
John is fishing.

Ruff liegt auf dem Boden.
Ruff is lying on the floor.

1. fireman: **der Feuermann.** 2. This word is singular in German.

| flour | das Mehl | fog | der Nebel | forest | der Wald |

Bill siebt das Mehl.
Bill is sifting the flour.

Henry hat sich im Nebel verlaufen.
Henry is lost in the fog.

Im Wald wachsen viele Bäume.
Many trees grow in the forest.

| to flow | fließen | to follow | folgen | to forget | vergessen |

Der Fluß fließt in das Meer.
The river flows into the sea.

Henry folgt einem Hund.
Henry is following a dog.

Bill hat meinen Namen vergessen.
Bill has forgotten my name.

Ich habe vergessen, wo er wohnt.
I have forgotten where he lives.

Vergiß uns nicht!
Don't forget us!

| flower | die Blume | food | das Essen | fork | die Gabel |

Henry gibt Fifi eine Blume.
Henry gives Fifi a flower.

Jake ißt das ganze Essen.
Jake eats all the food.

Ben hält eine Gabel in der Hand.
Ben is holding a fork.

| fly | die Fliege | for | für | fox | der Fuchs |

Eine Fliege sitzt auf der Blume.
There is a fly on the flower.

Das Geschenk ist für Ben.
The present is for Ben.

Der Fuchs ist rot.
The fox is red.

| to fly | fliegen | forehead | die Stirn | to freeze | gefrieren einfrieren |

Jetzt fliegt die Fliege.
Now the fly is flying.

Henry stößt sich die Stirn.
Henry hits his forehead.

Wenn Wasser gefriert, wird es zu Eis.
When water freezes, it turns into ice.

Fifi friert Essen in der Gefriertruhe ein.
Fifi freezes food in the freezer.

| French fries | die Pommes frites | in front of | vor | full of | voll |

Ben hat einen Teller Pommes frites.*
Ben has a plate of French fries.

Ben steht vor Bill.
Ben is standing in front of Bill.

Die Badewanne ist voll Wasser.
The bathtub is full of water.

| friend | der Freund die Freundin | frost | der Rauhreif[1] | funny | lustig |

Sam und Fifi sind Freunde.*
Sam and Fifi are friends.

Auf dem Fenster ist Rauhreif.
There is frost on the window.

Der Clown ist lustig.
The clown is funny.

| to frighten | erschrecken | fruit | das Obst | fur | das Fell |

Fifi erschreckt ihren Freund.
Fifi frightens her friend.

Viele Obstsorten.
Many kinds of fruit.

Das Kaninchen hat ein weißes Fell.
The rabbit has white fur.

| frog | der Frosch | fry | braten |

Der Frosch springt.
The frog is jumping.

Ben brät ein Ei.
Ben is frying an egg.

G g

| from | aus, von | frying pan | die Bratpfanne | game | das Spiel |

Der Brief kommt aus Frankreich.
The letter is from France.

Er ist von Pierre an Fifi.
It is from Pierre to Fifi.

Eier in einer Bratpfanne.
Eggs in a frying pan.

Ein Blinde Kuh Spiel.
A game of blindman's buff.

1. frost on the ground: **der Frost.**

garage **die Werkstatt**	gate **das Tor**	girl **das Mädchen**

Das Auto ist in der Werkstatt. The car is in the garage.	**Der Bauer schließt das Tor.** The farmer shuts the gate.	**Das Mädchen jagt eine Katze.** The girl is chasing a cat.

garbage can **die Mülltonne**	to get up **aufstehen**	to give **geben**

Bill schaut in die Mülltonne. Bill looks in the garbage can.	**Ben steht um 7 Uhr auf.** Ben gets up at 7 o'clock.	**Das Mädchen gibt Ben eine Blume.** The girl gives Ben a flower.

garden **der Garten**	ghost **das Gespenst**	glass **das Glas**

Im Garten wachsen Blumen. Flowers grow in the garden.	**Das Gespenst erschreckt Henry.** The ghost frightens Henry.	**Das Glas ist voll Milch.** The glass is full of milk.

gas **das Gas**	giant **der Riese**	glasses **die Brille**[1]

Henry zündet das Gas auf dem Herd an. Henry lights the gas stove.	**Der Riese ist ein sehr großer Mann.** The giant is a very big man.	**Henry trägt eine Brille.** Henry is wearing glasses.

gasoline **das Benzin**	giraffe **die Giraffe**	glove **der Handschuh**

Henry tankt Benzin. Henry puts gasoline in his car.	**Die Giraffe frißt Blätter.** The giraffe is eating leaves.	**Ein Paar rote Handschuhe. *** A pair of red gloves.

go **gehen**	**grape** **die Weintraube**	**grocer** **der Lebensmittel-händler**

Die Kinder gehen zur Schule.
The children go to school.

Hier sind Weintrauben.*
Here are some grapes.

Das ist ein Lebensmittelhändler.
This is a grocer.

goat **die Ziege**	**grapefruit** **die Pampelmuse**	**ground** **der Boden**

Die Ziege beißt Henry.
The goat bites Henry.

Fifi ißt eine Pampelmuse.
Fifi eats grapefruit.

Zizi sitzt auf dem Boden.
Zizi is sitting on the ground.

gold **das Gold**	**grass** **das Gras**	**group** **die Gruppe**

Fifis Kette ist aus Gold.
Fifi's chain is made of gold.

Ruff wälzt sich im Gras.
Ruff is rolling in the grass.

Hier ist eine Gruppe von Jungen.
Here is a group of boys.

good **gut**	**gray** **grau**	**to grow** **wachsen**

Ben ist ein guter Bäcker.
Ben is a good baker.

Die große Katze ist grau.
The big cat is gray.

Zizi wächst.
Zizi is growing.

goose **die Gans**	**green** **grün**	**guest** **der Gast**

Die Gans jagt die Ziege.
The goose chases the goat.

Das Gras ist grün.
The grass is green.

Fifi heißt den Gast willkommen.
Fifi welcomes the guest.

33

guitar	die Gitarre

Manuel spielt Gitarre.[1]
Manuel is playing the guitar.

gun	die Pistole

Sam schießt mit der Pistole.
Sam shoots the gun.

hair	das Haar

Oma hat weißes Haar.
Grandma has white hair.

hairbrush	die Haarbürste

Oma hat eine rosa Haarbürste.
Grandma has a pink hairbrush..

---

hairdresser	der Friseur

Der Friseur schneidet die Haare.
The hairdresser cuts hair.

half	halb

Zizi hat die halbe Orange.
Zizi has half the orange.

ham	der Schinken

Bill schneidet den Schinken.
Bill is cutting the ham.

hamburger	der Hamburger

Sam hat gerade zwei Hamburger* bestellt.
Sam just ordered two hamburgers.

hammer	der Hammer

Henry benutzt den Hammer.
Henry is using the hammer.

---

hand	die Hand

Henry schlägt auf seine Hand.
Henry hits his hand.

handbag	die Handtasche

Fifi hat eine rote Handtasche.
Fifi has a red handbag.

handkerchief	der Taschen-tuch

Fifi winkt mit ihrem Taschentuch.
Fifi waves her handkerchief.

handle	der Griff

Der Griff bricht ab.
The handle breaks.

to hang	hängen

Henry hängt am Seil.
Henry is hanging from a rope.

to happen   passieren

Wann ist der Unfall passiert?
When did the accident happen?

Wie ist das passiert?
How did it happen?

happy   glücklich

Bill ist glücklich.
Bill is happy.

harbor   der Hafen

Die Boote liegen im Hafen.
The boats are in the harbor.

hard   hart

Die Matratze ist hart.
The mattress is hard.

hat   der Hut

Fifi trägt einen hübschen Hut.
Fifi is wearing a pretty hat.

to have   haben

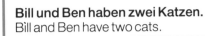

Bill und Ben haben zwei Katzen.
Bill and Ben have two cats.

hay   das Heu

Georg mäht das Gras und macht Heu.
George cuts grass to make hay.

head   der Kopf

Henry hat einen Vogel auf dem Kopf.
Henry has a bird on his head.

headlight   der Scheinwerfer

Die Scheinwerfer* brennen.
The headlights are shining.

to hear   hören

Opa kann nicht gut hören.
Grandpa cannot hear well.

heart   das Herz

Wenn man läuft, schlägt das Herz schneller.
When you run, your heart beats faster.

Ich liebe dich von ganzem Herzen.
I love you with all my heart.

heavy   schwer

Der Stein ist schwer.
The rock is heavy.

hedge   die Hecke

Henry schneidet die Hecke.
Henry is cutting the hedge.

helicopter   der Hub-schrauber

Der Hubschrauber fliegt.
The helicopter is flying.

to help   helfen

Bill hilft Ben.
Bill is helping Ben.

hen	das Huhn

Das Huhn frißt Körner.
The hen is eating seeds.

hill	der Hügel

Das Haus steht auf einem Hügel.
The house is on a hill.

homework	die Hausauf-gaben *

Tim macht seine Hausaufgaben. *
Tim is doing his homework.

here	hier hierher

Ich bleibe hier.
I am staying here.

Ich wohne hier.
I live here.

Komm hierher.
Come here.

hippopotamus	das Nilpferd

Das Nilpferd ist schmutzig.
The hippopotamus is muddy.

honey	der Honig

Der Honig ist im Topf.
The honey is in the jar.

to hide	sich verstecken

Der Dieb versteckt sich.
The thief is hiding.

to hit	schlagen

Zizi schlägt Ruff.
Zizi hits Ruff.

hook	der Haken

Der Hut hängt am Haken.
The hat is hanging on a hook.

high	hoch

Der Berg ist hoch.
The mountain is high.

to hold	halten

Die Hexe hält einen Besen in der Hand.
The witch is holding a broom in her hand.

to hop	hüpfen

Das Kaninchen hüpft über Ruff.
The rabbit hops over Ruff.

high	hoch

Der Vogel fliegt hoch am Himmel.
The bird is high in the sky.

hole	das Loch

Ruff gräbt ein Loch.
Ruff is digging a hole.

horse	das Pferd

Henry reitet auf einem Pferd.
Henry is riding a horse.

hospital das Krankenhaus

Henry ist im Krankenhaus.
Henry is in the hospital.

hot heiß

Die Suppe ist heiß.
The soup is hot.

hot dog das Würstchen

Fifi ißt ein Würstchen.
Fifi is eating a hot dog.

hotel das Hotel

Fifi geht in ein Hotel.
Fifi is going to a hotel.

hour die Stunde

Ein Tag hat 24 Stunden.*
There are 24 hours in a day.

Eine Stunde hat 60 Minuten.
There are 60 minutes in an hour.

house das Haus

Fritz wohnt in einem großen Haus.
Fritz lives in a big house.

how wie

Wie geht es dir?
How are you?

Wie bäckst du einen Kuchen?
How do you make a cake?

Wie sagst du das auf Deutsch?
How do you say it in German?

to be hungry hungrig

Zizi ist hungrig.
Zizi is hungry.

to hurry schnell laufen

Henry läuft schnell.
Henry is hurrying.

to hurt verletzen

Henry verletzte sich[1] den Fuß mit einem Stein.
Henry hurt his foot with a rock.

husband der Mann

Fritz ist Heidis Mann.
Fritz is Heidi's husband.

ice das Eis

Der Teich ist mit Eis bedeckt.
The pond is covered with ice.

ice cream das Eis

Zizi ißt ein Eis.
Zizi is eating ice cream.

idea die Idee

Was für eine gute Idee!
What a good idea!

Ich habe eine Idee.
I have an idea.

---

1. **sich** is used here because Henry has hurt a part of his own body.

37

if	**wenn**	instead of	**anstatt**	island	**die Insel**

if   **wenn**
ob

Komm, wenn du kannst.
Come if you can.

Er wird dir helfen, wenn du ihn darum bittest.
He will help you if you ask him.

Fifi fragt, ob Sam zu Hause ist.
Fifi asks if Sam is at home.

instead of   **anstatt**

Fifi ißt Honig anstatt Zucker.
Fifi eats honey instead of sugar.

Er spielt anstatt zu arbeiten.
He is playing instead of working.

island   **die Insel**

Eine Insel im Meer.
An island in the sea.

---

ill   **krank**

Bill ist krank.
Bill is ill.

intersection   **die Kreuzung**

Henry bleibt an der Kreuzung stehen.
Henry stops at the intersection.

---

important   **wichtig**

Der Präsident ist eine wichtige Person.
The President is an important person.

Es ist wichtig, daß du kommst.
It is important that you come.

to invite   **einladen**

Fifi lädt 20 Leute zu ihrer Party ein.
Fifi is inviting 20 people to her party.

jacket   **die Jacke**

Fritz hat eine grüne Jacke.
Fritz has a green jacket.

---

in   **in**

Die Katze liegt in dem Korb.
The cat is lying in the basket.

iron   **das Bügeleisen**

Das ist ein Bügeleisen.
This is an iron.

jam   **die Marmelade**[1]

Ein Glas Erdbeermarmelade.
A jar of strawberry jam.

---

insect   **das Insekt**

Das sind Insekten. *
These are insects.

to iron   **bügeln**

Henry bügelt sein Hemd.
Henry is ironing his shirt.

jar   **das Glas**

Das ist ein leeres Glas.
This is an empty jar.

---

1. The German for "marmalade" is **die Orangenmarmelade.**

jeans　　　die Jeans[1]

Das ist eine Jeans.
This is a pair of jeans.

jewels　　　der Schmuck

Der Einbrecher sieht den Schmuck.
The burglar sees the jewels.

to join　　　verbinden

Bill verbindet zwei Drähte.
Bill joins two wires.

joke　　　der Witz

Bill erzählt Ben einen Witz.
Bill tells Ben a joke.

to jump　　　springen

Ein Frosch springt.
One frog is jumping.

kangaroo　　　das Känguruh

Das Känguruh hüpft.
The kangaroo is jumping.

to keep　　　behalten
aufheben

Fifi möchte das Kleid behalten.
Fifi wants to keep the dress.

Ben behält sein altes Auto.
Ben is keeping his old car.

Hebe etwas Brot für morgen auf.
Keep some bread for tomorrow.

kettle　　　der Wasserkessel

Das Wasser im Wasserkessel kocht.
The water in the kettle is boiling.

key　　　der Schlüssel

Der Schlüssel hängt am Haken.
The key is on the hook.

---

to kick　　　treten

Sam tritt den Ball.
Sam kicks the ball.

to kill　　　töten

Der Prinz tötet den Drachen.
The prince kills the dragon.

kind　　　nett

Jim ist nett zu Tieren.
Jim is kind to animals.

kind　　　die Sorte
die Art

Äpfel sind eine Obstsorte.
Apples are a kind of fruit.

Zwiebeln sind eine Gemüsesorte.
Onions are a kind of vegetable.

Was für eine Art von Kuchen ist das?
What kind of cake is it?

king　　　der König

Der König trägt eine Krone.
The king is wearing a crown.

---

1. This is singular in German.

39

to kiss — küssen

Fifi küßt Sam.
Fifi is kissing Sam.

kitchen — die Küche

Ben kocht in der Küche.
Ben cooks in the kitchen.

kite — der Drachen

Bill läßt einen Drachen fliegen.
Bill is flying a kite.

kitten — das Kätzchen

Das Kätzchen spielt mit einer Maus.
The kitten is playing with a mouse.

knapsack — der Schulranzen

Terry hat einen roten Schulranzen.
Terry has a red knapsack.

knee — das Knie

Henry fällt auf das Knie.
Henry falls on his knee.

knife — das Messer

Bill schneidet mit einem Messer Brot.
Bill cuts bread with a knife.

to knit — stricken

Henry strickt.
Henry is knitting.

knitting — die Strickarbeit

Das ist seine Strickarbeit.
This is his knitting.

to knock — klopfen

Sam klopft an die Tür.
Sam knocks on the door.

knot — der Knoten

Der Faden hat einen Knoten.
The string has a knot in it.

to know (things) — wissen
(people) — kennen

Ich weiß, daß zwei und zwei vier sind.
I know that two and two are four.
Sam kennt Ben.
Sam knows Ben.

know how to — können

Fritz kann schwimmen.
Fritz knows how to swim.

lace — die Spitze

Das Kleid ist aus Spitze.
The dress is made of lace.

ladder — die Leiter

Henry klettert auf die Leiter.
Henry climbs the ladder.

lake	**der See**

Auf dem See sind Boote.
There are boats on the lake.

lamb	**das Lamm**

Ein Lamm ist ein junges Schaf.
A lamb is a baby sheep.

lamp	**die Lampe**

Fifi liest im Schein der Lampe.
Fifi is reading by the lamp.

last	**letzter/e/es**

Ben ist der letzte in der Schlange.
Ben is last in line.

to last	**dauern**
	anhalten

Der Film dauert eine Stunde.
The movie lasts an hour.

Wie lange wird es dauern?
How long will it last?

Das gute Wetter hielt fünf Tage an.
The good weather lasted for five days.

late	**spät**

Tim kommt zu spät zur Schule.
Tim is late for school.

Er geht spät ins Bett.
He goes to bed late.

Komme ich zu spät, um den Film zu sehen?
Am I too late for the movie?

to laugh	**lachen**

Ben lacht Bill aus.
Ben is laughing at Bill.

lawn	**der Rasen**

Fifi mäht den Rasen.
Fifi is mowing the lawn.

lazy	**faul**

Markus ist faul.
Mark is lazy.

to lead	**führen**

Ben führt die Kinder.
Ben is leading the children.

leaf	**das Blatt**

Die Ameise trägt ein Blatt.
The ant is carrying a leaf.

to leak	**tropfen**

Bens Wasserhahn tropft.
Ben's faucet is leaking.

to lean	**sich lehnen**

Bruno lehnt sich an einen Zaun.
Bruno is leaning on a fence.

to learn	**lernen**

Fifi lernt Autofahren.
Fifi learns how to drive.

Ich lerne Französisch in der Schule.
I am learning French at school.

leash	**die Leine**

Der Hund ist an einer Leine.
The dog is on a leash.

leather	das Leder

Diese Tasche ist aus Leder.
This purse is made of leather.

to leave	verlassen

Fifi verläßt das Haus.
Fifi is leaving the house.

left	links

Fritz biegt links ab.
Fritz turns left.

leg	das Bein

Henry läuft auf einem Bein Rollschuh.
Henry is skating on one leg.

lemon	die Zitrone

Fifi schneidet eine Zitrone in zwei Hälften.
Fifi cuts a lemon in half.

---

lesson	die Unterrichts-stunde

Die Klasse hat eine Unterrichtsstunde.
The class is having a lesson.

letter	der Brief

Sam liest einen Brief.
Sam is reading a letter.

lettuce	der Salat

Die Raupe ißt gern Salat.
The caterpillar likes lettuce.

library	die Bücherei

Bill ist in der Bücherei.
Bill is in the library.

to lick	lecken

Zizi leckt ihr Eis.
Zizi licks her ice cream.

---

lid	der Deckel

Bill tut den Deckel auf das Glas.
Bill puts the lid on the jar.

life	das Leben

Schmetterlinge haben ein kurzes Leben.
Butterflies have a short life.

Das Leben hier ist sehr ruhig.
Life is very quiet here.

Er hat mir das Leben gerettet.
He saved my life.

to lift	hochheben

Der Kran hebt einen Wagen hoch.
The crane is lifting a car.

light	leicht

Die Tänzerin ist leicht.
The dancer is light.

light	das Licht

Das Licht ist an.
The light is on.

| to light | anzünden | lip | die Lippe | long | lang |

to light   **anzünden**

Fritz zündet ein Streichholz an.
Fritz lights a match.

lip   **die Lippe**

Der Clown hat große, rote Lippen.*
The clown has big red lips.

long   **lang**

Die Schlange ist lang.
The snake is long.

lighthouse   **der Leuchtturm**

Der Leuchtturm steht am Meer.
The lighthouse is by the sea.

list   **die Liste**

Henry schreibt eine lange Liste.
Henry is writing a long list.

to look at   **sich ansehen**

Fifi sieht sich ein Bild an.
Fifi is looking at a picture.

lightning   **der Blitz**

Ein Blitz zuckt am Himmel auf.
Lightning flashes in the sky.

to listen   **hören**[1]

Opa hört Radio.
Grandpa listens to the radio.

to look for   **suchen**

Henry sucht ein Buch.
Henry is looking for a book.

to like   **mögen**

Fifi mag Ben.
Fifi likes Ben.

to live   **leben**

Rob lebt auf einer Insel.
Rob lives on an island.

to get lost   **sich verfahren**[2]

Henry hat sich verfahren.
Henry is lost.

lion   **der Löwe**

Der Löwe brüllt.
The lion is roaring.

living room   **das Wohnzimmer**

Das ist ein Wohnzimmer.
This is a living room.

a lot of   **eine Menge**

Es sind eine Menge Vögel in dem Baum.
There are a lot of birds in the tree.

---

1. "To listen" is normally **zuhören** but **Radio hören** means "to listen to the radio."   2. When you are walking "lost" is **"verlaufen."**   43

loud — **laut**

Die Kapelle spielt laut.
The band plays loud music.

to love — **lieben**

Sam liebt Fifi.
Sam loves Fifi.

low — **niedrig**

Die Mauer ist niedrig.
The wall is low.

lunch — **das Mittagessen**

Zizi ißt ihr Mittagessen.
Zizi eats lunch.

machine — **die Maschine**

Alle diese Maschinen* funktionieren.
All these machines work.

magazine — **die Zeitschrift**

Henry liest eine Zeitschrift.
Henry is reading a magazine.

magician — **der Zauberer**

Ein Zauberer und sein Kaninchen.
A magician and his rabbit.

mailman — **der Postbote**

Der Postbote bringt Briefe.
The mailman brings letters.

to make — **machen**

Ben macht einen Teig.
Ben is making dough.

man — **der Mann**

Ein Mann und zwei Frauen.
One man and two women.

many — **viele**

Der Mann verkauft viele Zeitschriften.
The man sells many magazines.

map — **die Landkarte**

Henry schaut auf einer Landkarte nach.
Henry looks at a map.

mark — **das Zeichen**

Auf der Landkarte ist ein Zeichen.
There is a mark on the map.

(open-air) market — **der Markt**

Das ist ein Markt.
This is an open-air market.

to marry **heiraten**	medicine **die Medizin**	middle **die Mitte**

Sam heiratet Fifi.
Sam is marrying Fifi.

Eine Krankenschwester gibt Zizi Medizin.
A nurse gives Zizi medicine.

Das Schwein steht in der Mitte.
The pig is standing in the middle.

mask **die Maske**	to meet **treffen**	milk **die Milch**

Wer trägt die Maske?
Who is wearing the mask?

Bill trifft Ben.
Bill meets Ben.

Zizi trinkt Milch.
Zizi is drinking milk.

match **das Streichholz**	to melt **schmelzen**	minute **die Minute**

Fred zündet ein Streichholz an.
Fred lights a match.

Das Eis schmilzt.
The ice cream is melting.

Eine Minute hat 60 Sekunden.
There are 60 seconds in a minute.

Eine Stunde hat 60 Minuten. *
There are 60 minutes in an hour.

to measure **messen**	menu **die Speisekarte**	mirror **der Spiegel**

Fifi mißt Zizi.
Fifi measures Zizi.

Fifi liest die Speisekarte.
Fifi reads the menu.

Die Katze sieht in den Spiegel.
The cat looks in the mirror.

meat **das Fleisch**	metal **das Metall**	to miss **verpassen**

Der Metzger hackt das Fleisch.
The butcher is chopping meat.

Ein Auto ist aus Metall.
A car is made of metal.

Henry verpaßt den Bus.
Henry misses the bus.

model	**das Modell**

Fritz baut ein Modellflugzeug.
Fritz is making a model airplane.

money	**das Geld**

Ben zählt sein Geld.
Ben is counting his money.

monkey	**der Affe**

Der Affe schaukelt.
The monkey is swinging.

monster	**das Ungeheuer**

Das Ungeheuer ist freundlich.
The monster is friendly.

month	**der Monat**

Ein Jahr hat zwölf Monate. *
There are twelve months in a year.

Der Januar ist der erste Monat im Jahr.
January is the first month of the year.

Der Dezember ist der letzte Monat im Jahr.
December is the last month of the year.

moon	**der Mond**

Der Mond steht am Himmel.
The moon is in the sky.

more	**mehr**

Bill hat mehr Geld als Ben.
Bill has more money than Ben.

morning	**der Morgen**
	morgens

Der Morgen kommt vor dem Mittag.
Morning comes before noon.

Morgens geht man zur Arbeit und zur Schule.
People go to work and to school in the morning.

most	**die meisten**

Die meisten dieser Äpfel sind rot.
Most of the apples are red.

mother	**die Mutter**

Mary ist Zizis Mutter.
Mary is Zizi's mother.

motorcycle	**das Motorrad**

Henry fährt Motorrad.
Henry is riding a motorcycle.

mountain	**der Berg**

Das ist ein hoher Berg.
This is a high mountain.

mouse	**die Maus**

Eine Maus ist rosa.
One mouse is pink.

mouth	**der Mund**

Der Mann hat einen großen Mund.
The man has a big mouth.

to move	**umstellen**

Sie stellen den Tisch um.
They are moving the table.

movie	**der Film**	music	**die Musik**	naughty	**ungezogen**

Fifi und Sam sehen einen Film.
Fifi and Sam watch a movie.

Eine Kapelle macht Musik.
A band plays music.

Zizi ist ungezogen.
Zizi is naughty.

movie theater	**das Kino**	mustache	**der Schnurr-bart**	near	**nahe**

Fifi ist im Kino.
Fifi is at the movie theater.

Der Mann hat einen Schnurrbart.
The man has a mustache.

Der Baum steht nahe am Haus.
The tree is near the house.

much	**viel**			neck	**der Hals**

Hast du viel Geld?
Do you have much money?

Mir geht es heute viel besser.
I feel much better today.

Eine Giraffe hat einen langen Hals.
A giraffe has a long neck.

mud	**der Schlamm**	nail	**der Nagel**	necklace	**die Kette**

Ein Ungeheuer spielt im Schlamm.
A monster is playing in the mud.

Henry trifft einen Nagel.
Henry hits a nail.

Fifi trägt eine Kette.
Fifi is wearing a necklace.

mushroom	**der Pilz**	name	**der Name**	to need	**nötig haben**

Eine Maus auf einem Pilz.
A mouse on a mushroom.

Zizi schreibt ihren Namen.
Zizi writes her name.

Zizi hat ein Bad nötig.
Zizi needs a bath.

| needle — **die Nadel** | next to — **neben** | nose — **die Nase** |

Fifi fädelt eine Nadel ein.
Fifi threads a needle.

Fifi sitzt neben Sam.
Fifi is sitting next to Sam.

Henry hat eine rote Nase.
Henry has a red nose.

| nest — **das Nest** | night — **die Nacht** | notebook — **das Notizbuch** |

Junge Vögel leben in einem Nest.
Baby birds live in a nest.

Es ist Nacht.
It is night.

Der Mann liest sein Notizbuch.
The man reads his notebook.

| never — **nie** | nobody — **niemand** | nothing — **nichts** |

Fifi ißt nie Käse.
Fifi never eats cheese.

Ich sehe nie fern.
I never watch television.

Opa geht nie aus.
Grandpa never goes out.

Niemand trägt einen Hut.
Nobody is wearing a hat.

Es ist nichts in der Schachtel.
There is nothing in the box.

| new — **neu** | noise — **der Lärm** | now — **jetzt** |

Ben hat ein neues Auto.
Ben has a new car.

Zizi macht Lärm.
Zizi is making noise.

Es ist jetzt 5 Uhr.
It is now 5 o'clock.

Ich komme jetzt.
I am coming now.

Ich gehe jetzt nach Hause.
Now I am going home.

| newspaper — **die Zeitung** | north — **der Norden** | number — **die Zahl** |

Bill liest eine Zeitung.
Bill is reading a newspaper.

Der Vogel blickt nach Norden.
The bird is facing north.

Dies sind alles Zahlen.*
These are all numbers.

| nurse | die Kranken-schwester | office | das Büro | onion | die Zwiebel |

Eine Krankenschwester gibt Ben Medizin.
A nurse gives Ben medicine.

Jake arbeitet in einem Büro.
Jake works in an office.

Henry schneidet Zwiebeln. *
Henry is slicing onions.

| nut | die Nuß | often | oft | only | nur |

Zizi ißt Nüsse. *
Zizi is eating nuts.

Das Telefon klingelt oft.
The telephone often rings.

Nur ein Schwein ist schwarz.
Only one pig is black.

| | | to oil | ölen | to open | öffnen |

Tim ölt sein Fahrrad.
Tim oils his bicycle.

Fifi öffnet die Tür.
Fifi opens the door.

| octopus | der Krake | old | alt | open | geöffnet |

Der Krake lebt in der See.
An octopus lives in the sea.

Opa ist ein alter Mann.
Grandpa is an old man.

Das Geschäft ist geöffnet.
The store is open.

| to offer | schenken | on | auf | opposite | das Gegenteil |

Sam schenkt Fifi Blumen.
Sam offers Fifi flowers.

Die Tasse steht auf dem Tisch.
The cup is on the table.

Heiß ist das Gegenteil von kalt.
Hot is the opposite of cold.

or **oder**	**out of** **aus . . . heraus**	**package** **das Paket**

or   **oder**

Welche Schuhe möchtest du haben? Die blauen oder die roten?
Which shoes do you want? The blue ones or the red ones?

Du kannst das eine oder das andere Paar haben.
You can have one pair or the other.

out of   **aus . . . heraus**

Das Spielzeug ist aus der Kiste heraus.
The toys are out of the box.

package   **das Paket**

Der Postbote bringt ein Paket.
The mailman brings a package.

---

orange   **orangefarbig**

Henry hat orangefarbige Socken.
Henry has orange socks.

outside   **draußen**

Zizi spielt draußen.
Zizi is playing outside.

page   **die Seite**

Das ist die erste Seite.
This is the first page.

---

orange   **die Apfelsine**

Eine Apfelsine ist orange.
An orange is orange.

over   **über**

Das Schwein springt über den Zaun.
The pig jumps over the fence.

to paint   **malen**

Die Künstlerin malt.
The artist is painting.

---

to order   **bestellen**

Fritz bestellt das Essen.
Fritz orders dinner.

owl   **die Eule**

Die Eule sitzt im Baum.
The owl is in the tree.

paints   **die Farben***

Das sind ihre Farben.*
These are her paints.

---

other   **anderer/e/es**

Wo ist die andere Socke?
Where is the other sock?

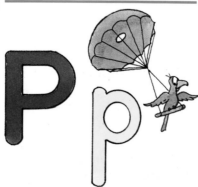

pair   **das Paar**

Ein Paar orangefarbige Socken.
A pair of orange socks.

palace	parents	to pass by
der Palast	**die Eltern***	**vorbeigehen**

palace **der Palast**

Der König wohnt in einem Palast.
The king lives in a palace.

parents **die Eltern***

Zizi ist bei ihren Eltern.*
Zizi is with her parents.

to pass by **vorbeigehen**

Henry geht an Bruno vorbei.
Henry passes Bruno by.

pancake **der Pfannkuchen**

Bill bäckt einen Pfannkuchen.
Bill is making a pancake.

park **der Park**

Fifi geht im Park spazieren.
Fifi is walking in the park.

passport **der Paß**

Ben zeigt seinen Paß.
Ben shows his passport.

pants **die Hose**

Ben hat eine rote Hose an.
Ben has red pants on.

to park **parken**

Henry parkt sein Auto.
Henry is parking his car.

path **der Weg**

Der Weg geht quer durch das Feld.
The path crosses the field.

paper **das Papier**

Zizi malt auf Papier.
Zizi is painting on paper.

parrot **der Papagei**

Der Papagei lacht.
The parrot is laughing.

patient **der Patient**

Der Patient liegt im Bett.
The patient is in bed.

parachute **der Fallschirm**

Der Fallschirm kommt herunter.
The parachute is coming down.

party **die Party**

Fifi feiert eine Party.
Fifi is giving a party.

paw **die Pfote**

Die Katze leckt ihre Pfote.
The cat is licking its paw.

to pay **bezahlen**	pencil **der Bleistift**	piano **das Klavier**

Fifi bezahlt das Brot.
Fifi pays for the bread.

Sie zeichnet mit einem Bleistift.
She draws with a pencil.

Fritz spielt Klavier.
Fritz plays the piano.

pea **die Erbse**	people **die Leute***	to pick **pflücken**

Zizi ißt Erbsen.*
Zizi is eating peas.

Diese Leute* reden.
These people are talking.

Die Leute pflücken Birnen.
The people are picking pears.

peach **der Pfirsich**	pepper **der Pfeffer**	to pick up **aufheben**

Bill ißt einen Pfirsich.
Bill is eating a peach.

Bill streut Pfeffer auf sein Essen.
Bill puts pepper on his food.

Fifi hebt eine Birne auf.
Fifi picks up a pear.

pear **die Birne**	perhaps **vielleicht**	picnic **das Picknick**

Vielleicht wird es regnen.
Perhaps it will rain.

Vielleicht hat er sich verlaufen.
Perhaps he is lost.

Ben ißt eine Birne.
Ben is eating a pear.

Die Freunde machen ein Picknick.
The friends are having a picnic.

pen **der Füllfederhalter**	photograph **das Foto**	picture **das Bild**

Fifi schreibt mit einem Füllfederhalter.
Fifi writes with a pen.

Das ist ein Foto von Fifi.
This is a photograph of Fifi.

Ein Bild von einem Picknick.
A picture of a picnic.

52

pie **der Obstkuchen**	pilot **der Pilot**	pipe **die Pfeife**

pie **der Obstkuchen**

Bill schneidet den Obstkuchen.
Bill cuts the pie.

pilot **der Pilot**

Ein Pilot fliegt ein Flugzeug.
A pilot flies an airplane.

pipe **die Pfeife**

Ben raucht eine Pfeife.
Ben is smoking a pipe.

piece **das Stück**

Zizi ißt ein Stück Obstkuchen.
Zizi eats a piece of pie.

pin **die Stecknadel**

Bill sticht Ben mit einer Stecknadel.
Bill sticks Ben with a pin.

pitcher **der Krug**

Fifi gießt Milch aus einem Krug.
Fifi pours milk from a pitcher.

pig **das Schwein**

Das ist ein rosa Schwein.
This is a pink pig.

to pinch **kneifen**

Bill kneift Ben.
Bill pinches Ben.

place **der Platz**
der Ort

Ben sucht nach einem Picknickplatz.
Ben is looking for a place to have a picnic.

Sie wohnt an einem schönen Ort.
She lives in a pretty place.

pile **der Stapel**

Henry hat einen Stapel Bücher.
Henry has a pile of books.

pineapple **die Ananas**

Eine große Ananas.
A big pineapple.

plant **die Pflanze**

Henry hat eine Pflanze.
Henry has a plant.

pillow **das Kopfkissen**

Zizi hat ein weiches Kopfkissen.
Zizi has a soft pillow.

pink **rosa**

Das große Schwein ist rosa.
The big pig is pink.

to plant **pflanzen**

Er pflanzt sie in den Garten.
He plants it in the garden.

plate	**der Teller**

Die Pommes frites sind auf einem Teller.
The French fries are on a plate.

to play	**spielen**

Die Kinder spielen.
The children are playing.

pocket	**die Tasche**

Das Taschentuch ist in seiner Tasche.
The handkerchief is in his pocket.

to point	**zeigen**

Ben zeigt auf Bill.
Ben is pointing at Bill.

policeman	**der Polizist**

Der Polizist zeigt.
The policeman is pointing.

to polish	**polieren**

Fritz poliert den Tisch.
Fritz is polishing the table.

polite	**höflich**

Bill ist sehr höflich.
Bill is very polite.

Es ist höflich "bitte" zu sagen, wenn man um etwas bittet.
It is polite to say "Please" when you ask for something.

pond	**der Teich**

Die Enten schwimmen auf einem Teich.
Ducks are swimming in a pond.

pony	**das Pony**

Henry reitet auf einem Pony.
Henry is riding a pony.

poor	**arm**

Ein armer Mann hat wenig Geld.
A poor man has little money.

porcupine	**der Igel**

Das ist ein Igel.
This is a porcupine.

pork	**das Schweinefleisch**

Fritz ißt Schweinefleisch.
Fritz is eating pork.

port	**der Hafen**

Das Schiff liegt im Hafen.
The ship is in port.

postcard	**die Postkarte**

Fifi schreibt eine Postkarte.
Fifi writes a postcard.

post office	**die Post**

Fifi ist bei der Post.
Fifi is at the post office.

pot **der Topf**	pretty **hübsch**	to pull **ziehen**

Ben hebt den Topf hoch.
Ben picks up the pot.

Fifi ist ein hübsches Mädchen.
Fifi is a pretty girl.

Bill und Ben ziehen am Seil.
Bill and Ben are pulling the rope.

potato **die Kartoffel**	price **der Preis**	puppet **die Marionette**

Henry schält eine Kartoffel.
Henry peels a potato.

Welchen Preis zahlt man für Kartoffeln?
What is the price of potatoes?

Die Marionette tanzt.
The puppet is dancing.

to pour **eingießen**	prize **der Preis**	puppy **das Hündchen**

Henry gießt Saft ein.
Henry is pouring juice.

Henry gewinnt einen Preis.
Henry wins a prize.

Ein Hündchen spielt mit dem Ball.
A puppy is playing with the ball.

present **das Geschenk**	to promise **versprechen**	purple **lila**

Henry gibt Fifi ein Geschenk.
Henry gives Fifi a present.

Fifi verspricht, Henry eine Postkarte zu schicken.
Fifi promises to send Henry a postcard.

Ich verspreche dir, daß ich komme.
I promise you that I will come.

Der König trägt einen lila Mantel.
The king has a purple coat.

to pretend **so tun, als ob**	pudding **der Pudding**	purse **das Portemonnaie**

Fifi tut so, als ob sie ein Gespenst sei.
Fifi pretends to be a ghost.

Zizi ißt gerne Pudding.
Zizi likes to eat pudding.

Fifi tut Geld in ihr Portemonnaie.
Fifi puts money in her purse.

55

| to push | **stoßen** | queen | **die Königin** | rabbit | **das Kaninchen** |

Bill stößt Ben.
Bill is pushing Ben.

Die Königin trägt eine Krone.
The queen wears a crown.

Das Kaninchen läuft.
The rabbit is running.

---

to put **stellen**

Fifi stellt Milch in den Kühlschrank.
Fifi puts milk in the refrigerator.

question **die Frage**

Die Königin stellt eine Frage.
The queen asks a question.

Bitte beantworte meine Frage.
Please answer my question.

Es gibt keine Antwort auf die Frage.
The question has no answer.

to race **rennen**

Die Kaninchen rennen um die Wette.
The rabbits are racing.

---

puzzle **das Puzzle**

Fritz macht ein Puzzle.
Fritz is doing a puzzle.

quiet **leise**

Der Einbrecher ist sehr leise.
The burglar is very quiet.

radiator **der Heizkörper**

Ein Heizkörper erwärmt einen Raum.
A radiator warms a room.

---

pyjamas **der Schlafanzug**[1]

Henry trägt einen Schlafanzug.
Henry is wearing pyjamas.

quite **ziemlich**

Der Film ist ziemlich gut, aber das Buch ist besser.
The movie is quite good, but the book is better.

Er ist ziemlich klug.
He is quite smart.

radio **das Radio**

Opa hört Radio.
Grandpa is listening to the radio.

---

railroad track **das Bahngleis**

Ein Kaninchen sitzt auf dem Bahngleis.
A rabbit is sitting on the railroad track.

1. This is singular in German.

to rain **regnen**	**razor** **der Rasierapparat**	**to recognize** **erkennen**

Fritz erkennt Fifi.
Fritz recognizes Fifi.

Ich erkenne ihre Schrift.
I recognize her handwriting.

Es regnet.
It is raining.

Sam rasiert sich mit einem Rasierapparat.
Sam shaves with a razor.

rainbow **der Regenbogen**	**to reach** **herankommen**	**record** **die Schallplatte**

Ein Regenbogen am Himmel.
A rainbow in the sky.

Fifi kommt nicht an das Buch heran.
Fifi cannot reach the book.

Bill legt eine Schallplatte auf.
Bill puts on a record.

raincoat **der Regenmantel**	**to read** **lesen**	**red** **rot**

Henry trägt einen Regenmantel.
Henry is wearing a raincoat.

Fifi liest ein Buch.
Fifi is reading a book.

Fifi malt den Stuhl rot an.
Fifi is painting the chair red.

raspberry **die Himbeere**	**real** **echt**	**refrigerator** **der Kühlschrank**

Eine Schüssel voll Himbeeren.*
A dish of raspberries.

Das ist ein echter Elefant.
This is a real elephant.

Ben stellt Milch in den Kühlschrank.
Ben puts milk in the refrigerator.

rat **die Ratte**	**to receive** **erhalten**	**to refuse** **sich weigern**

Die Ratte jagt ein Kaninchen.
The rat is chasing a rabbit.

Fifi erhält einen Brief.
Fifi receives a letter.

Der Esel weigert sich weiterzugehen.
The donkey refuses to move.

to remember sich erinnern

Fritz erinnert sich an Fifi.
Fritz remembers Fifi.

Henry kann sich nicht erinnern, wo sein Buch ist.
Henry cannot remember where his book is.

to ride reiten

Henry reitet auf einem Esel.
Henry is riding a donkey.

road die Straße

Auf der Straße stehen Schafe.
There are sheep on the road.

to rest sich ausruhen

Henry ruht sich aus.
Henry is resting.

right recht

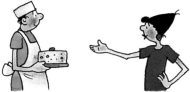

Fifi streckt ihre rechte Hand aus.
Fifi raises her right hand.

to roar brüllen

Der Löwe brüllt.
The lion is roaring.

ribbon die Schleife

Zizi hat eine blaue Schleife im Haar.
Zizi has a blue ribbon in her hair.

ring der Ring

Ein Ring an seiner rechten Hand.
A ring on his right hand.

rock der Felsen

Henry sitzt auf einem Felsen.
Henry is sitting on a rock.

rice der Reis

Die Chinesen essen gerne Reis.
The Chinese like to eat rice.

to ring klingeln

Das Telefon klingelt.
The telephone is ringing.

roof das Dach

Das Haus hat ein rotes Dach.
The house has a red roof.

rich reich

Das ist ein reicher Mann.
This is a rich man.

river der Fluß

Der Fluß ist breit.
The river is wide.

room das Zimmer

Das ist ein Zimmer in Fifis Haus.
This is a room in Fifi's house.

rooster	**der Hahn**	round	**rund**		

Der Hahn kräht.
The rooster is calling.

Der Tisch ist rund.
The table is round.

root	**die Wurzel**	row	**die Reihe**	sack	**der Sack**

Die Pflanze hat lange Wurzeln.*
The plant has long roots.

Fünf Schweine in einer Reihe.
Five pigs in a row.

Der Dieb trägt einen Sack.
The thief is carrying a sack.

rope	**das Seil**	to row	**rudern**	sad	**traurig**

Henry klettert an einem Seil hoch.
Henry is climbing a rope.

Bill rudert ein Boot.
Bill is rowing a boat.

Henry ist traurig.
Henry is sad.

rose	**die Rose**	to rub	**reiben**	safe	**sicher**

Fifi riecht an einer Rose.
Fifi is smelling a rose.

Die Katze reibt ihren Rücken.
The cat is rubbing its back.

Henry hat einen sicheren Platz.
Henry is in a safe place.

rough	**uneben**	to run	**laufen**	to sail	**segeln**

Die Straße ist uneben.
The road is rough.

Henry läuft weg.
Henry is running away.

Fifi segelt auf einem Segelboot.
Fifi is sailing a boat.

sailboat **das Segelboot**	sand **der Sand**	sausage **das Würstchen**

Das Segelboot ist auf See.
The sailboat is at sea.

Zizi gräbt im Sand.
Zizi is digging in the sand.

Ben ißt Würstchen.*
Ben is eating sausages.

sailor **der Matrose**	sandal **die Sandale**	saw **die Säge**

Der Matrose steuert ein Boot.
The sailor is sailing a boat.

Ein Paar Sandalen.*
A pair of sandals.

Bill sägt Holz mit einer Säge.
Bill cuts wood with a saw.

salad **der Salat**	sandwich **das Butterbrot**	to say **sagen**

Ein Salat besteht aus Gemüse.
A salad is made of vegetables.

Ein sehr dickes Butterbrot.
A very big sandwich.

Bill sagt, daß er reich ist.
Bill says he is rich.

Sie sagt, daß sie kommen.
She says they are coming.

salt **das Salz**	sauce **die Soße**	scale **die Waage**

Bill streut Salz auf den Salat.
Bill puts salt on the salad.

Fifi gießt die Soße darüber.
Fifi is pouring the sauce.

Fifi steht auf der Waage.
Fifi stands on the scale.

same **gleich**	saucer **die Untertasse**	scarf **der Schal**

Zwei Mädchen mit dem gleichen Hut.
Two girls with the same hat.

Die Tasse steht auf einer Untertasse.
The cup is on a saucer.

Henry hat einen sehr langen Schal.
Henry has a very long scarf.

school	die Schule	to see	sehen	sentence	der Satz

Die Kinder sind in der Schule.
The children are at school.

Zizi kann den Seehund sehen.
Zizi can see the seal.

Das ist ein Satz.
This is a sentence.

scissors	die Schere[1]	seed	der Same	to serve	bedienen

Fifi schneidet die Haare mit einer Schere.
Fifi cuts hair with scissors.

Dan sät Samen.*
Dan is planting seeds.

Der Kellner bedient Fifi.
The waiter is serving Fifi.

to scratch	kratzen	to seem	scheinen	to sew	nähen

Ruff kratzt sich am Ohr.
Ruff is scratching his ear.

Er scheint böse zu sein.
He seems to be angry.

Henry näht.
Henry is sewing.

sea	das Meer	to sell	verkaufen	sewing machine	die Näh-maschine

Das Meer ist blau.
The sea is blue.

Der Bäcker verkauft Brot.
The baker sells bread.

Er benutzt eine Nähmaschine.
He is using a sewing machine.

seal	der Seehund	to send	schicken	shadow	der Schatten

Der Seehund schwimmt im Meer.
The seal is in the sea.

Fifi schickt einen Brief.
Fifi is sending a letter.

Zizi betrachtet ihren Schatten.
Zizi is looking at her shadow.

1. This is a singular noun in German.

to shake	schütteln	shed	die Hütte	shirt	das Hemd

Bill schüttelt den Baum.
Bill is shaking the tree.

Ein Mann steht in der Hütte.
A man is standing in the shed.

Fritz hat ein blaues Hemd.
Fritz has a blue shirt.

shape	die Form	sheep	das Schaf	shoe	der Schuh

Das sind verschiedene Formen.*
These are different shapes.

Drei Schafe* in einer Reihe.
Three sheep in a row.

Ein Paar rote Schuhe.*
A pair of red shoes.

to share	teilen	sheet	das Bettlaken	short	kurz

Bill und Ben teilen den Kuchen.
Bill and Ben share the cake.

Fifi tut ein Bettlaken auf das Bett.
Fifi puts a sheet on the bed.

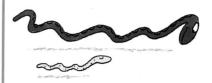

Die gelbe Schlange ist kurz.
The yellow snake is short.

shark	der Hai	shell	die Muschel	shorts	die Shorts*

Der Hai verfolgt Henry.
The shark is chasing Henry.

Zizi hebt eine Muschel auf.
Zizi picks up a shell.

Henry hat weiße Shorts* an.
Henry has white shorts.

sharp	scharf	ship	das Schiff	shoulder	die Schulter

Das Messer ist scharf.
The knife is sharp.

Das Schiff ist auf hoher See.
The ship is at sea.

Auf Bobs Schulter sitzt ein Vogel.
A bird is sitting on Bob's shoulder.

| shovel **die Schaufel** | sidewalk **der Bürgersteig** | sink **das Waschbecken** |

Dan gräbt mit einer Schaufel.
Dan is digging with a shovel.

Fifi ist auf dem Bürgersteig.
Fifi is on the sidewalk.

Das Waschbecken ist gelb.
The sink is yellow.

to show **zeigen**

Fifi zeigt Opa ihr Bild.
Fifi shows Grandpa her picture.

sign **die Warnung²**

Fred liest eine Warnung.
Fred is reading a sign.

sister **die Schwester**

Zizi und Daisy sind Schwestern.*
Zizi and Daisy are sisters.

to shower **duschen¹**

Henry duscht.
Henry is taking a shower.

silver **silbern**

Fifi hat einen silbernen Armreifen.
Fifi has a silver bracelet.

to sit **sitzen**

Zizi sitzt auf einem Stuhl.
Zizi is sitting on a chair.

shut **zu**

Das Tor ist zu.
The gate is shut.

since **seit da**

Fifi hat Ben seit Dienstag nicht gesehen.
Fifi has not seen Ben since Tuesday.

Da es sonnig ist, gehe ich spazieren.
Since it is sunny, I will go for a walk.

to skate **Schlittschuh laufen**

Fifi und Henry laufen Schlittschuh.
Fifi and Henry are skating.

side **die Seite**

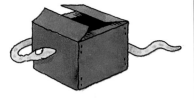

Eine Seite der Schachtel ist rosa.
One side of the box is pink.

to sing **singen**

Die Leute singen.
The people are singing.

ski **der Schi**

Henry schnallt seine Schier* an.
Henry puts on skis.

1. The verb **"duschen"** means "to take a shower." 2. "Sign" can also be **"Mitteilung"** or **"Hinweis"** but here it's "warning."

63

to ski **Schi laufen**	sleeve **der Ärmel**	slowly **langsam**

Henry läuft Schi.
Henry is skiing.

Das Hemd hat nur einen Ärmel.
The shirt only has one sleeve.

Eine Schnecke bewegt sich langsam.
A snail moves slowly.

skin **die Haut**	slice **die Scheibe**	small **klein**

Ein Elefant hat graue Haut.
An elephant has gray skin.

Bill schneidet eine Scheibe Brot.
Bill cuts a slice of bread.

Der braune Bär ist klein.
The brown bear is small.

skirt **der Rock**	to slide **rutschen**	to smell **riechen**

Fifi trägt einen roten Rock.
Fifi is wearing a red skirt.

Henry rutscht auf dem Eis.
Henry is sliding on the ice.

Fifi riecht das Parfüm.
Fifi smells the perfume.

sky **der Himmel**	slide **das Dia**	to smile **lächeln**

Der Vogel fliegt am Himmel.
The bird is in the sky.

Das ist ein Dia.
This is a slide.

Fifi lächelt.
Fifi is smiling.

to sleep **schlafen**	slipper **der Pantoffel**	to smoke **rauchen**

Zizi schläft.
Zizi is sleeping.

Zizi hat rote Pantoffeln.*
Zizi has red slippers.

Opa raucht eine Pfeife.
Grandpa is smoking a pipe.

snail	die Schnecke

Hier ist die Schnecke wieder.
Here is the snail again.

snake	die Schlange

Die Schlange ist im Gras.
The snake is in the grass.

to snow	schneien

Es schneit.
It is snowing.

soap	die Seife

Ben hat Seife im Gesicht.
Ben has soap on his face.

soccer	der Fußball

Sam spielt Fußball.
Sam is playing soccer.

sock	die Socke

Zizi trägt rosa Socken.*
Zizi is wearing pink socks.

sofa	das Sofa

Fifi sitzt auf dem Sofa.
Fifi is sitting on a sofa.

soft	weich

Das Kissen ist weich.
The cushion is soft.

soldier	der Soldat

Der Soldat ist in der Armee.
The soldier is in the army.

some	einige

Einige Soldaten lächeln.
Some soldiers are smiling.

someone	jemand

Jemand hat mein Auto gestohlen.
Someone has stolen my car.

something	etwas

Ich habe etwas im Auge.
There is something in my eye.

sometimes	manchmal

Manchmal bin ich traurig.
Sometimes I am sad.

son	der Sohn

Henry ist Opas Sohn.
Henry is Grandpa's son.

song	das Lied

Die Sängerin singt ein Lied.
The singer is singing a song.

soon	bald

Wir gehen bald nach Hause.
We will go home soon.

Ich möchte so bald wie möglich gehen.
I want to go as soon as possible.

sort	die Art

Drei Arten* von Hüten.
Three sorts of hats.

soup **die Suppe**	to spend **ausgeben**	square **das Quadrat**

Henry ißt Suppe.
Henry is eating soup.

Ben gibt Geld aus.
Ben is spending money.

Das ist ein Quadrat.
This is a square.

south **der Süden**	spider **die Spinne**	stable **der Stall**

Der Vogel blickt nach Süden.
The bird is facing south.

Die Spinne erschreckt Fifi.
The spider frightens Fifi.

Das Pferd wohnt in einem Stall.
The horse lives in a stable.

space **der Weltraum**	spoon **der Löffel**	stairs **die Treppe**[1]

Der Astronaut ist im Weltraum.
The astronaut is in space.

Zizi ißt mit einem Löffel.
Zizi is eating with a spoon.

Zizi geht die Treppe hinauf.
Zizi is going up the stairs.

to speak **sprechen**	spot **der Fleck**	stamp **die Briefmarke**

Fifi spricht mit Opa.
Fifi is speaking to Grandpa.

Zizi hat viele Flecken.*
Zizi has lots of spots.

Zwei Briefmarken* auf einem Umschlag.
Two stamps on an envelope.

to spell **buchstabieren**	to spread **streichen**	to stand **stehen**

Zizi kann ihren Namen buchstabieren.
Zizi can spell her name.

Bill streicht die Butter auf das Brot.
Bill is spreading the butter.

Bill steht auf Ben.
Bill is standing on Ben.

star	**der Stern**	to steal	**stehlen**	stocking	**der Strumpf**

Der Stern leuchtet am Himmel.
The star shines in the sky.

Fred stiehlt Schmuck.
Fred is stealing jewelry.

Fifi hat schwarze Strümpfe* an.
Fifi has black stockings.

---

to start	**anfangen**	stem	**der Stengel**	stone	**der Stein**

Das Rennen fängt an.
The race is starting.

Die Blume hat einen langen Stengel.
The flower has a long stem.

Zizi hebt einen Stein auf.
Zizi picks up a stone.

---

station	**der Bahnhof**	steps	**die Stufen***	to stop	**halten**

Ein Zug steht im Bahnhof.
A train is in the station.

Die Katze sitzt auf den Stufen.*
The cat is sitting on the steps.

Das Auto hält am Fußgängerüberweg.
The car stops at the crossing.

---

statue	**die Statue**	stereo	**die Stereoanlage**	store	**das Geschäft**

Henry sieht sich eine Statue an.
Henry is looking at a statue.

Das ist eine Stereoanlage.
This is a stereo.

Fifi geht in ein Geschäft.
Fifi goes into a store.

---

to stay	**bleiben**	stick	**der Stock**	storm	**das Gewitter**

Bleib hier!
Stay here!

Fifi bleibt im Bett.
Fifi is staying in bed.

Dan trägt Stöcke.*
Dan is carrying sticks.

Das ist ein Gewitter.
This is a storm.

67

story **die Geschichte**

Opa liest eine Geschichte.
Grandpa is reading a story.

street **die Straße**

Das ist eine Straße in einer Stadt.
This is a street in a town.

submarine **das Untersee-boot**

Das Unterseeboot ist unter Wasser.
The submarine is underwater.

stove **der Herd**

Sein Herd ist sehr alt.
His stove is very old.

string **der Bindfaden**

Ein Stück Bindfaden.
A piece of string.

subway **die U-Bahn**

Eine U-Bahn-Station.
A subway station.

straight **gerade**

Die Straße ist sehr gerade.
The road is very straight.

striped **gestreift**

Fifi hat ein gestreiftes Kleid an.
Fifi has a striped dress.

suddenly **plötzlich**

Das Auto hält plötzlich.
The car stops suddenly.

strawberry **die Erdbeere**

Zizi ißt eine Erdbeere.
Zizi is eating a strawberry.

strong **stark**

Sam ist stark.
Sam is strong.

sugar **der Zucker**

Fifi tut Zucker in ihren Tee.
Fifi puts sugar in her tea.

stream **der Bach**

Fifi durchquert einen Bach.
Fifi is crossing a stream.

stupid **dumm**

Henry kommt sich dumm vor.
Henry is feeling stupid.

suit **der Anzug**

Henry trägt einen Anzug.
Henry is wearing a suit.

suitcase	**der Koffer**

Ben trägt einen Koffer.
Ben is carrying a suitcase.

to swallow	**schlucken**

Die Schlange schluckt etwas.
The snake swallows something.

swimsuit	**der Badeanzug**

Fifi trägt einen gestreiften Badeanzug.
Fifi is wearing a striped swimsuit.

sun	**die Sonne**

Die Sonne scheint.
The sun is shining.

swan	**der Schwan**

Der Schwan schwimmt.
The swan is swimming.

swing	**die Schaukel**

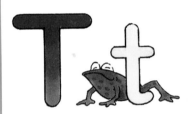

Ben ist auf einer Schaukel.
Ben is on a swing.

supermarket	**der Super-markt**

Fifi ist im Supermarkt.
Fifi is at the supermarket.

sweater	**die Strickjacke**

Aggie trägt eine rosa Strickjacke.
Aggie is wearing a pink sweater.

T t

surprise	**die Überraschung**

Was für eine Überraschung für Fifi!
What a surprise for Fifi!

to swim	**schwimmen**

Bill und Ben schwimmen.
Bill and Ben are swimming.

table	**der Tisch**

Die Katze sitzt auf dem Tisch.
The cat is on the table.

to surround	**um . . . herum stehen**

Die Vögel stehen um die Katze herum.
The birds surround the cat.

swimming pool	**das Schwimm-bad**

Das ist das Schwimmbad.
This is the swimming pool.

tail	**der Schwanz**

Nur eine Katze hat einen Schwanz.
Only one cat has a tail.

to take / nehmen

Zizi nimmt eine Praline.
Zizi is taking a chocolate.

tall / groß

Die Frau ist groß.
The woman is tall.

to taste / probieren

Ben probiert die Soße.
Ben is tasting the sauce.

taxi / das Taxi

Fritz ruft ein Taxi.
Fritz calls a taxi.

tea / der Tee

Fifi trinkt eine Tasse Tee.
Fifi has a cup of tea.

teacher / der Lehrer[1]

Der Lehrer unterrichtet die Klasse.
The teacher is teaching the class.

team / die Mannschaft

Eine Fußballmannschaft.
A soccer team.

teapot / die Teekanne

Fifi gießt den Tee aus der Teekanne.
Fifi pours tea from a teapot.

to tear / zerreißen

Henry zerreißt seine Hose.
Henry tears his pants.

tear / die Träne

Zizi hat Tränen* im Gesicht.
Zizi has tears on her face.

teddy bear / der Teddybär

Zizi hat einen Teddybär.
Zizi has a teddy bear.

teeth / die Zähne[2]*

Die Ratte hat scharfe Zähne.*
The rat has sharp teeth.

telephone / das Telefon

Das Telefon klingelt.
The telephone is ringing.

television / das Fernsehen

Die Kinder sehen eine Sendung im Fernsehen.
The children watch a television program.

to tell / erzählen

Opa erzählt den Kindern eine Geschichte.
Grandpa is telling the children a story.

1. A lady teacher: **die Lehrerin.**   2. tooth: **der Zahn.**

tennis	das Tennis	then	dann	thing	das Ding

tennis — **das Tennis**

Die Männer spielen Tennis.
The men are playing tennis.

then — **dann**

Er aß sein Essen, dann ein Stück Kuchen.
He ate his dinner, then he had a piece of cake.

Kleb eine Briefmarke auf den Brief, dann schick ihn ab.
Put a stamp on the letter, then mail it.

thing — **das Ding**

Zehn Dinge* auf einem Tablett.
Ten things on a tray.

---

tent — **das Zelt**

Henry schaut aus dem Zelt heraus.
Henry looks out of the tent.

there — **da**

Das Auto ist nicht da.
The car is not there.

Ist Fifi da?
Is Fifi there?

Geh nicht da weg.
Do not move from there.

to think — **denken**

Fifi denkt an Sam.
Fifi is thinking about Sam.

---

to thank — **danken**

Fifi dankt Ben für das Geschenk.
Fifi thanks Ben for the present.

thick — **dick**

Die Scheibe Brot ist dick.
The slice of bread is thick.

to be thirsty — **durstig**

Der Mann ist durstig.
The man is thirsty.

---

that — **der/die/das . . . da**

Gib mir den Apfel da.
Give me that apple.

Ich möchte den Apfel da, nicht diesen hier.
I would like that apple, not this one.

thief — **der Einbrecher**

Der Einbrecher stiehlt Schmuck.
The thief is stealing jewels.

this — **dieser/e/es dies**

Nimm diesen Hut hier, nicht den da.
Take this hat, not that one.

Dies hier ist ein Elefant, und das da ist ein Kamel.
This is an elephant and that is a camel.

---

theater — **das Theater**

Fifi ist im Theater.
Fifi is at the theater.

thin — **dünn**

Der Mann ist dünn.
The man is thin.

thread — **das Garn**

Fifis Garn ist aus Baumwolle.
Fifi's thread is made of cotton.

through	**durch**	to tie	**knüpfen**	to	**zu**

Der König kommt durch die Tür herein.
The king comes through the door.

Bill knüpft einen Knoten.
Bill is tying a knot.

Die Kinder gehen zur Schule.
The children go to school.

Fifi geht zur Arbeit.
Fifi is going to work.

Henry geht zum Bahnhof.
Henry is going to the train station.

---

to throw	**werfen**	tiger	**der Tiger**	today	**heute**

Zizi wirft den Enten Brot zu.
Zizi is throwing bread to the ducks.

Der Tiger brüllt.
The tiger is roaring.

Heute ist Zizis Geburtstag.
Today is Zizi's birthday.

---

thumb	**der Daumen**	tights	**die Strumpfhose**[1]	toe	**die Zehe**

Henry haut sich auf den Daumen.
Henry hits his thumb.

Eine rote Strumpfhose.
A pair of red tights.

Ein Fuß hat fünf Zehen. *
A foot has five toes.

---

ticket	**die Fahrkarte**	tire	**der Reifen**	together	**zusammen**

Fifi zeigt ihre Fahrkarte.
Fifi shows her ticket.

Das Fahrrad hat platte Reifen. *
The bicycle has flat tires.

Die Katzen schlafen zusammen.
The cats sleep together.

---

tie	**die Krawatte**	tired	**müde**	tomato	**die Tomate**

Henry hat eine gepunktete Krawatte.
Henry has a spotted tie.

Henry ist müde.
Henry is tired.

Henry schneidet Tomaten. *
Henry is slicing tomatoes.

1. This is singular in German.

| tomorrow | morgen | toothpaste | die Zahnpasta | tower | der Turm |

Morgen ist der Tag nach heute.
Tomorrow is the day after today.

Heute ist Montag, also ist morgen Dienstag.
Today is Monday so tomorrow will be Tuesday.

Zahnpasta auf einer Zahnbürste.
Toothpaste on a toothbrush.

Wo steht dieser berühmte Turm?
Where is this famous tower?

| tongue | die Zunge | top | oben | town | die Stadt |

Ruff hat eine rosa Zunge.
Ruff has a pink tongue.

Ben steht oben auf der Leiter.
Ben is at the top of the stepladder.

Das ist eine Stadt.
This is a town.

| too | zu | to touch | berühren | toy | das Spielzeug |

Die Jacke ist zu klein.
The coat is too small.

Der Polizist berührt den Einbrecher.
The policeman touches the thief.

Zizi spielt mit einem Spielzeug.
Zizi is playing with a toy.

| tool | das Werkzeug | towards | auf ... zu | tractor | der Traktor |

Das sind alles Werkzeuge.*
These are all tools.

Die Katze geht auf die Milch zu.
The cat is going towards the milk.

Henry fährt einen Traktor.
Henry is driving a tractor.

| toothbrush | die Zahnbürste | towel | das Handtuch | traffic light | die Ampel |

Eine gelbe Zahnbürste.
A yellow toothbrush.

Henry hat ein gelbes Handtuch.
Henry has a yellow towel.

Er fährt gegen die Ampel.
He hits the traffic light.

trailer **der Wohnwagen**	truck **der Lastwagen**	to type **Schreibmaschine schreiben**

Fred hat einen großen Wohnwagen.
Fred has a big trailer.

Henry fährt einen Lastwagen.
Henry is driving a truck.

Henry schreibt Schreibmaschine.
Henry is typing.

train **der Zug**	trumpet **die Trompete**	typewriter **die Schreibmaschine**

Henry steigt in den Zug ein.
Henry gets on the train.

Ben spielt Trompete.
Ben is playing a trumpet.

Die Schreibmaschine ist sehr alt.
The typewriter is very old.

treasure **der Schatz**	tulip **die Tulpe**	

Ali Baba findet einen Schatz.
Ali Baba finds treasure.

Die Tulpen* stehen in einer Vase.
The tulips are in a vase.

tree **der Baum**	to turn **abbiegen**	ugly **häßlich**

Der Baum hat grüne Blätter.
The tree has green leaves.

Das Auto biegt links ab.
The car is turning left.

Das Ungeheuer ist häßlich.
The monster is ugly.

triangle **das Dreieck**	twin **der Zwilling**	umbrella **der Regenschirm**

Das sind alles Dreiecke.*
These are all triangles.

Bella und Betty sind Zwillinge.*
Bella and Betty are twins.

Henry verliert seinen Regenschirm.
Henry loses his umbrella.

74

uncle	der Onkel

Tom ist Zizis Onkel.
Tom is Zizi's uncle.

under	unter

Die Katze ist unter dem Bett.
The cat is under the bed.

to understand	verstehen

Ich verstehe, was er sagt.
I understand what he says.

Ich verstehe, wie diese Maschine funktioniert.
I understand how this machine works.

Ich verstehe Französisch.
I understand French.

to undress	ausziehen

Fifi zieht Zizi aus.
Fifi is undressing Zizi.

unhappy	unglücklich

Henry ist unglücklich.
Henry is unhappy.

until	bis

Ben ist bis morgen zu Hause.
Ben is at home until tomorrow.

Warte, bis ich zurückkomme.
Wait until I come back.

up	hinauf

Henry klettert die Leiter hinauf.
Henry is going up a ladder.

upstairs	oben

Die Katze ist oben.
The cat is upstairs.

to use	benutzen

Fifi benutzt ein Messer.
Fifi is using a knife.

useful	nützlich

Das Messer ist nützlich.
The knife is useful.

V v

vacation	der Urlaub

Bill ist in Urlaub.
Bill is on vacation.

vacuum cleaner	der Staub- sauger

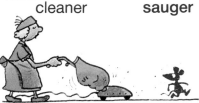

Ein blauer Staubsauger.
A blue vacuum cleaner.

valley	das Tal

Ein Fluß in einem Tal.
A river in a valley.

van	der Kleinbus

Henry fährt einen Kleinbus.
Henry is driving a van.

vase **die Vase**

Die Vase ist voll Blumen.
The vase is full of flowers.

vegetables **die Gemüse***

Das sind Gemüse.*
These are all vegetables.

very **sehr**

Das Mädchen ist sehr hübsch.
The girl is very pretty.

Henry spricht sehr gut Französisch.
Henry speaks French very well.

Sehr gut!
Very good!

village **das Dorf**

Ein Dorf ist kleiner als eine Stadt.
A village is smaller than a town.

violin **die Geige**

Henry spielt Geige.
Henry plays the violin.

to visit **besuchen**

Fifi besucht Opa.
Fifi is visiting Grandpa.

voice **die Stimme**

Opa hat eine leise Stimme.
Grandpa has a quiet voice.

Ben hat eine tiefe Stimme, und Fifi hat eine hohe Stimme.
Ben has a low voice and Fifi has a high voice.

to wait **warten**

Aggie wartet auf einen Bus.
Aggie is waiting for a bus.

waiter **der Kellner**

Der Kellner bedient Fifi.
The waiter serves Fifi.

to wake up **aufwachen**

Henry wacht auf.
Henry is waking up.

walk **der Spaziergang**

Fifi macht einen Spaziergang.
Fifi is going for a walk.

wall **die Mauer**

Die Katzen sitzen auf der Mauer.
The cats are on the wall.

wallpaper **die Tapete**

Die Tapete fällt von der Wand.
The wallpaper is falling off.

to want **wollen**

Zizi will ein Törtchen.
Zizi wants a cupcake.

| war | der Krieg | watch | die Uhr | to wear | tragen |

war — **der Krieg**

Die beiden Länder führen Krieg.
The two countries are at war.

Der Krieg dauert schon zwei Jahre.
The war has lasted two years.

watch — **die Uhr**

Fifi sieht auf ihre Uhr.
Fifi looks at her watch.

to wear — **tragen**

Fifi trägt einen Hut.
Fifi is wearing a hat.

warm — **warm**

Fifi ist es warm.
Fifi is warm.

water — **das Wasser**

Die Badewanne ist voll Wasser.
The bathtub is full of water.

wedding — **die Hochzeit**

Eine Hochzeit in der Kirche.
A wedding at the church.

to wash — **waschen**

Henry wäscht sein Gesicht.
Henry is washing his face.

waterfall — **der Wasserfall**

Tarzan überquert den Wasserfall.
Tarzan crosses the waterfall.

to weigh — **abwiegen**

Fifi wiegt das Mehl ab.
Fifi is weighing the flour.

washing machine — **die Waschmaschine**

Die Waschmaschine läuft.
The washing machine is on.

wave — **die Welle**

Ben springt in die Welle.
Ben dives under the wave.

west — **der Westen**

Der Vogel blickt nach Westen.
The bird is facing west.

wasp — **die Wespe**

Die Wespe sticht Henry.
The wasp stings Henry.

weak — **schwach**

Henry ist schwach.
Henry is weak.

wet — **naß**

Der Hund ist naß.
The dog is wet.

what — was

Was möchtest du zum Mittagessen?
What would you like for lunch?

Was sagst du? Ich verstehe nicht.
What are you saying? I do not understand.

wheat — der Weizen

Der Weizen wächst auf dem Feld.
Wheat is growing in the field.

wheel — das Rad

Ein Fahrrad hat zwei Räder. *
A bicycle has two wheels.

wheelbarrow — der Schub-karren

Der Schubkarren ist voll.
The wheelbarrow is full.

when — wann als wenn

Wann fährt der letzte Zug?
When does the last train leave?

Ich hatte ein Auto, als ich in Paris wohnte.
I had a car when I lived in Paris.

Komm, wenn du fertig bist.
Come when you have finished.

where — wo

Wo ist die Katze?
Where is the cat?

which — welcher/e/es

Welche Katze ist am größten?
Which cat is the biggest?

while — während

Zizi träumt, während sie schläft.
Zizi dreams while she sleeps.

to whisper — flüstern

Fifi flüstert Ben etwas zu.
Fifi is whispering to Ben.

whistle — die Trillerpfeife

Der Mann bläst auf einer Trillerpfeife.
The man is blowing a whistle.

white — weiß

Die dicke Katze ist weiß.
The fat cat is white.

who — wer

Wer trägt einen Hut?
Who is wearing a hat?

why — warum

Warum hängt Henry im Baum?
Why is Henry up a tree?

wide — breit

Der Fluß ist sehr breit.
The river is very wide.

wife — die Frau

Heidi ist die Frau von Fritz.
Heidi is Fritz's wife.

| to win | **gewinnen** | to wipe | **abwischen** | woman | **die Frau** |

Sam gewinnt das Rennen.
Sam wins the race.

Bill wischt den Tisch ab.
Bill is wiping the table.

Fifi ist eine Frau. Henry ist ein Mann.
Fifi is a woman. Henry is a man.

| wind | **der Wind** | wire | **der Draht** | wood | **das Holz** |

Der Wind bläst.
The wind is blowing.

Der Zaun ist aus Draht.
The fence is made of wire.

Der Tisch ist aus Holz.
The table is made of wood.

| windmill | **die Windmühle** | witch | **die Hexe** | wool | **die Wolle** |

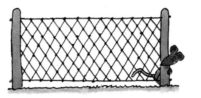

Das ist eine Windmühle.
This is a windmill.

Die Hexe fliegt.
The witch is flying.

Drei Knäuel Wolle.
Three balls of wool.

| window | **das Fenster** | with | **mit** | word | **das Wort** |

Der Einbrecher zerschlägt das Fenster.
The thief breaks the window.

Die Hexe mit ihrer Katze.
The witch with her cat.

Zizi schreibt ein Wort.
Zizi is writing a word.

| wing | **der Flügel** | without | **ohne** | to work | **arbeiten** |

Der Vogel flattert mit den Flügeln.*
The bird flaps its wings.

Die Hexe ohne ihre Katze.
The witch without her cat.

Ben arbeitet tüchtig.
Ben is working hard.

workbook das Übungsheft

Tim schreibt in sein Übungsheft.
Tim is writing in his workbook.

world die Welt

Diese Karte zeigt die ganze Welt.
This map shows the whole world.

worm der Wurm

Der Vogel sieht sich den Wurm an.
The bird looks at the worm.

to wrap einwickeln

Fifi wickelt ein Geschenk ein.
Fifi is wrapping a present.

to write schreiben

Fifi schreibt einen Brief.
Fifi is writing a letter.

wrong falsch

Die Antwort ist falsch.
The answer is wrong.

year das Jahr

Ein Jahr hat 365 Tage.
There are 365 days in a year.

Ein Jahr hat 12 Monate oder 52 Wochen.
There are 12 months or 52 weeks in a year.

to yell schreien

Ben schreit.
Ben is yelling.

yellow gelb

Das Küken ist gelb.
The chick is yellow.

yesterday gestern

Gestern war der Tag vor heute.
Yesterday was the day before today.

Heute ist Montag, gestern war Sonntag.
Today is Monday, yesterday was Sunday.

young jung

Ein Welpe ist ein junger Hund.
A puppy is a young dog.

zebra das Zebra

Ein Zebra hat ein gestreiftes Fell.
A zebra has a striped coat.

zoo der Zoo

Zizi sieht ein Zebra im Zoo.
Zizi sees a zebra at the zoo.

Pronunciation Guide

The best way to learn to speak German is to listen carefully to German-speaking people and copy what they say, but here are some general pointers to help you.

Below is a list of letters that sound different in German from the way they sound in English, with a guide to show you how to say each one. For each German word, we show an English word (or part of a word) that sounds like it. Read it out loud normally to find out how to pronounce the German sound, then practice saying the examples shown below.

a
When it is short, it is like the "a" in "cat":
d**a**nke, T**a**sse, St**a**dt, B**a**ll

When it is long, it is like the "ar" sound in "cart":
V**a**ter, f**a**hren, B**a**hnhof

ä
Like the "a" in "care":
sp**ä**t, L**ä**rm, K**ä**se, B**ä**r

au
Like the "ow" sound in "cow":
Fr**au**, **au**f, b**au**en

äu, eu
Like the "oy" sound in "toy":
Fr**äu**lein, Fr**eu**nd, h**eu**te

ö
Like the "u" sound in "fur":
öffnen, h**ö**ren, m**ö**chte, zw**ö**lf

ü
Round your lips as if you were going to say "oo," then try to say "ee":
über, f**ü**r, k**ü**ssen, T**ü**r

ei
Like the "i" in "fine":
n**ei**n, G**ei**ge, M**ei**sten, R**ei**he

ie
Like the "ee" sound in "feel":
T**ie**r, s**ie**ben, fl**ie**gen, Sp**ie**l

ch
A soft sound like the "ch" in the composer's name "Bach":
i**ch**, Bu**ch**, ma**ch**en, a**ch**t

d
Like the English "d" – except at the end of a word, where it is "t":
dort, **D**ing, un**d**, Mon**d**, Gel**d**

g
Like the "g" in "garden" – except after "i," where it is like the German "ch" above:
Geld, **G**arten, We**g**, schmutzi**g**

j
Like the "y" in "yellow":
ja, **J**unge, **J**acke

sch
Like the "sh" sound in "shirt":
schön, **Sch**okolade, **sch**nell

sp, st
These sound like "shp" and "sht" when they are at the beginning of a word:
Spiegel, **sp**rechen, **St**uhl, **St**adt

s
Like "z" when it comes before a vowel:
sehen, **s**itzen, **S**and, lang**s**am

Before other letters, it is like the "s" in "soap":
Wü**s**te, Li**s**te, etwa**s**, Ne**s**t

ß
This is like "ss":
Pa**ß**, Stra**ß**e

v
Like the "f" in "friend":
von, **v**iel, **V**ater

w
Like the "v" in "van":
Wasser, **w**arm, **w**er, **W**ort

z
Like the "ts" in "hits":
zu, Her**z**, **z**usammen, **Z**unge

Basic Grammar

German grammar is different from English grammar. These notes will help you understand some of the things you come across in this dictionary. Do not worry if you do not understand everything at first.

Nouns

In German all nouns begin with a capital letter and they are all either masculine, feminine, or neuter. The word you use for "the" shows which gender the noun is, so you should learn which word for "the" to use with each noun. The word for "the" is **der** before masculine (m) nouns, **die** before feminine (f) nouns, and **das** before neuter (n) nouns.

der Hund	the dog
die Blume	the flower
das Buch	the book

The word for "the" is **die** before all plural (pl) nouns.

die Hunde	the dogs
die Blumen	the flowers
die Bücher	the books

Most German nouns change their endings when they are plural. It is a good idea to learn the plural form of a word at the same time as the singular. You will find the plural forms of nouns listed in the index at the back of the dictionary.

You may come across other words for "the": **den, dem,** and **des**. But do not worry about these now. You will learn about them when you know more German.

a, an

The German for "a" or "an" is **ein** before masculine and neuter words and **eine** before feminine words.

ein Hund	a dog
eine Blume	a flower
ein Buch	a book

Pronouns

The German word for "it" depends on whether the noun it replaces is masculine, feminine or neuter.

der Hund schläft	the dog is sleeping
er schläft	it is sleeping

die Katze schläft	the cat is sleeping
sie schläft	it is sleeping

The subject pronouns in German are:

I	**ich**	we	**wir**
you (sing.)	**du**	you (pl)	**ihr**
he, it (m)	**er**	they	**sie**
she, it (f)	**sie**	you (polite)	**Sie**
it (n)	**es**		

Possessives

The ending of the word you use for "my," "your," "his," etc. changes, depending on whether the word that follows it is masculine, feminine, neuter, or plural. The words change in the same way as **ein, eine** above. Look at the examples on the right.

mein Hund (m)	my dog
meine Blume (f)	my flower
mein Buch (n)	my book
meine Hunde (pl)	my dogs
meine Blumen (pl)	my flowers
meine Bücher (pl)	my books

The possessives in German are:

	(m)	(f)	(n)	(pl)
my	**mein**	**meine**	**mein**	**meine**
your	**dein**	**deine**	**dein**	**deine**
his, its (m)(n)	**sein**	**seine**	**sein**	**seine**
her, its (f)	**ihr**	**ihre**	**ihr**	**ihre**
our	**unser**	**unsere**	**unser**	**unsere**
your	**ihr**	**ihre**	**ihr**	**ihre**
your (polite)	**Ihr**	**Ihre**	**Ihr**	**Ihre**
their	**ihr**	**ihre**	**ihr**	**ihre**

Adjectives

Adjectives that stand before nouns change their endings to go with the nouns they are describing. Below you can see what the basic endings are.

After der, die, and das

(m)	(f)	(n)	(pl)
der gute Mann	**die gute Frau**	**das gute Mädchen**	**die guten Männer/ Frauen/Mädchen**
the good man	the good women	the good girl	the good men/ women/girls

After ein, eine

(m)	(f)	(n)	(pl)
ein guter Mann	**eine gute Frau**	**ein gutes Mädchen**	**gute Männer/ Frauen/Mädchen**
a good man	a good woman	a good girl	good men/ women/girls

Verbs

The ending of a German verb changes depending on its subject. **Gehen** (to go) is an example of a typical verb with all the usual endings. The other three verbs below are useful ones to learn because they are used so much.

Du (singular) and **ihr** (plural) are used by close friends and children when they are speaking to each other. You use **Sie,** spelled with a capital "S," when speaking to people you do not know well.

gehen	to go	sein	to be
ich gehe	I go	ich bin	I am
du gehst	you go	du bist	you are
er/sie/es geht	he/she/it goes	er/sie/es ist	he/she/it is
wir gehen	we go	wir sind	we are
ihr geht	you go (pl)	ihr seid	you are (pl)
Sie gehen	you go (polite)	Sie sind	you are (polite)
sie gehen	they go	sie sind	they are

haben	to have	können	to be able to, can
ich habe	I have	ich kann	I can
du hast	you have	du kannst	you can
er/sie/es hat	he/she/it has	er/sie/es kann	he/she/it can
wir haben	we have	wir können	we can
ihr habt	you have (pl)	ihr könnt	you can (pl)
Sie haben	you have (polite)	Sie können	you can (polite)
sie haben	they have	sie können	they can

Separable verbs

When you are reading the German sentences in this dictionary you will notice that some of the verbs break up into two words. This is because they are made up of two words put together. For example, the verb "to arrive" is **ankommen,** made up of **an** (at) + **kommen** (to come). When the verb is used in a sentence it often splits into its two parts.

Der Zug kommt an   The train arrives

Useful Words and Phrases

Months, Seasons, and Days

The months

January	Januar
February	Februar
March	März
April	April
May	Mai
June	Juni
July	Juli
August	August
September	September
October	Oktober
November	November
December	Dezember

The seasons

spring	der Frühling
summer	der Sommer
autumn/fall	der Herbst
winter	der Winter

The days

Monday	Montag
Tuesday	Dienstag
Wednesday	Mittwoch
Thursday	Donnerstag
Friday	Freitag
Saturday	Samstag/Sonnabend
Sunday	Sonntag

Numbers and Telling Time

1 eins	12 zwölf	30 dreißig	102 hundertzwei
2 zwei	13 dreizehn	31 einunddreißig	110 hundertzehn
3 drei	14 vierzehn	32 zweiunddreißig	120 hundertzwanzig
4 vier	15 fünfzehn	40 vierzig	150 hundertfünfzig
5 fünf	16 sechzehn	50 fünfzig	200 zweihundert
6 sechs	17 siebzehn	60 sechzig	201 zweihunderteins
7 sieben	18 achtzehn	70 siebzig	202 zweihundertzwei
8 acht	19 neunzehn	80 achtzig	500 fünfhundert
9 neun	20 zwanzig	90 neunzig	1000 (ein)tausend
10 zehn	21 einundzwanzig	100 (ein)hundert	1100 tausendeinhundert
11 elf	22 zweiundzwanzig	101 hunderteins	5000 fünftausend

Telling time

What time is it, please?

It is nine o'clock.
It is five after nine.
It is a quarter after nine.
It is half past nine.
It is a quarter to ten.
It is five to ten.
It is noon/midnight.

Wie spät ist es, bitte?

Es ist neun Uhr.
Es ist fünf nach neun.
Es ist viertel nach neun.
Es ist halb zehn.
Es ist viertel vor zehn.
Es ist fünf vor zehn.
Es ist Mittag/Mitternacht.

Countries and Continents

Africa	Afrika	Great Britain	Großbritannien
Argentina	Argentinien	Hungary	Ungarn
Asia	Asien	India	Indien
Australia	Australien	Italy	Italien
Austria	Österreich	Japan	Japan
Belgium	Belgien	Mexico	Mexiko
Brazil	Brasilien	The Netherlands	die Niederlande
Canada	Kanada	North America	Nordamerika
China	China	Poland	Polen
Czechoslovakia	die Tschechoslovakei	South America	Südamerika
Denmark	Dänemark	Soviet Union	die Sowjetunion
England	England	Spain	Spanien
Europe	Europa	Switzerland	die Schweiz
France	Frankreich	United States	die Vereinigten Staaten
Germany	Deutschland	Yugoslavia	Yugoslawien

Useful Words and Phrases

Yes	Ja
No	Nein
Please	Bitte
I would like . . .	Ich möchte . . .
Thank you	Danke
I'm sorry	Es tut mir leid
Excuse me	Entschuldigung
Mr.	Herr
Mrs.	Frau
Miss	Fräulein
I do not understand.	Ich verstehe nicht.
I do not speak German.	Ich spreche kein Deutsch.
Please speak more slowly.	Langsamer bitte.

Asking directions

Where is . . . ?	Wo ist . . . ?
Where are . . . ?	Wo sind . . . ?
Can you help me?	Können Sie mir helfen?
How do I get to the train station please?	Wie komme ich bitte zum Bahnhof?
Turn right	Rechts abbiegen.
Turn left	Links abbiegen.
Go straight ahead	Immer geradeaus.
How far is it?	Wie weit ist es?

Making friends

Hello	Guten Tag
Good evening	Guten Abend
Good night	Gute Nacht
Goodbye	Auf Wiedersehen
What is your name?	Wie heißt du?
My name is Roger.	Ich heiße Roger.
How are you?	Wie geht's?
I am well, thank you.	Gut, danke.
Pleased to meet you.	Sehr erfreut.

Useful places to ask for

airport	der Flughafen
bank	die Bank
campsite	der Campingplatz
pharmacy	die Apotheke
hospital	das Krankenhaus
police station	die Polizeiwache
post office	das Postamt
train station	der Bahnhof
tourist office	das Verkehrsamt
youth hostel	die Jugendherberge

85

Index

To find out what the plural of a noun is, look at the letters in parentheses after it. (-) means that the noun does not change in the plural. (-e) or (-er) means that you add "e" or "er" to the end of a noun. (-) means that you add an umlaut to the main vowel in the noun, or to the main vowel in the last part if it is long, e.g. **der Vater** (-) becomes **die Väter** in the plural. **Das Schwimmbad** (-er) becomes **die Schwimmbäder**. Do not forget the word for "the" is **die** before all plural nouns (see page 82).

abbiegen	to turn	74
der Abend (-e)	evening	26
aber	but	14
abwiegen	to weigh	77
abwischen	to wipe	79
der Adler (-)	eagle	25
die Adresse (-n)	address	4
der Affe (-n)	monkey	46
alle	all	5
alle	everyone	27
allein	alone	5
das Alphabet (-e)	alphabet	5
als	as	7
als	when	78
alt	old	49
das Alter (-)	age	4
am	by	14
die Ameise (-n)	ant	6
die Ampel (-n)	traffic light	73
die Amsel (-n)	blackbird	10
an	against	4
die Ananas (-)	pineapple	53
and... /e/es	other	50
anfangen	to begin	9
anfangen	to start	67
angeln	to fish	29
die Angst (-e)	to be afraid	4
anhalten	to last	41
ankommen	to arrive	6
anstatt	instead of	38
anziehen	to dress	24
der Anzug (-e)	suit	68
anzünden	to light	43
der Apfel (-)	apple	6
die Apfelsine (-n)	orange	50
die Apotheke (-n)	drugstore	24
arbeiten	to work	79
arm	poor	54
der Arm (-e)	arm	6
das Armband (-er)	bracelet	12
die Armee (-n)	army	6
der Ärmel (-)	sleeve	64
die Art (-en)	kind	39
die Art (-en)	sort	65
der Arzt (-e)	(male) doctor	23
die Ärztin (-en)	(female) doctor	23
der Ast (-e)	branch	12
der Astronaut (-en)	astronaut	7
atmen	to breathe	12
auch	also	5
auf	on	49

auf ... zu	towards	73
aufheben	to keep	39
aufheben	to pick up	52
aufregend	exciting	27
aufstehen	to get up	32
aufwachen	to wake up	76
das Auge (-n)	eye	27
aus	from	31
aus ... heraus	out of	50
ausblasen	to blow out	11
ausgeben	to spend	66
ausschneiden	to cut out	21
außer	except	27
ausziehen	to undress	75
das Baby (-s)	baby	7
der Bach (-e)	stream	68
der Bäcker (-)	baker	7
der Badeanzug (-e)	swimsuit	69
die Badewanne (-n)	bathtub	8
das Badezimmer (-)	bathroom	8
das Bahngleis (-e)	railroad track	56
der Bahnhof (-e)	station	67
bald	soon	65
der Ball (-e)	ball	7
der Ballon (-s)	balloon	8
die Banane (-n)	banana	8
die Bank (-en)	bank	8
die Bank (-e)	bench	10
der Bär (-en)	bear	8
der Bart (-e)	beard	8
der Baseball	baseball	8
bauen	to build	13
der Bauer (-n)	farmer	28
der Bauernhof (-e)	farm	28
der Baum (-e)	tree	74
bedecken	to cover	20
bedienen	to serve	61
behalten	to keep	39
beide	both	11
das Bein (-e)	leg	42
beißen	to bite	10
bellen	to bark	8
benutzen	to use	75
das Benzin	gasoline	32
der Berg (-e)	mountain	46
berühmt	famous	27
berühren	to touch	73
beschäftigt	busy	14
beschreiben	to describe	22

besser	better	10	das Café (-s)	café	14
bestellen	to order	50	der Clown (-s)	clown	19
bester/e/es	best	10	das Comic (-s)	comic book	19
besuchen	to visit	76	der Computer (-)	computer	19
betreten	to enter	26	der Cowboy (-s)	cowboy	20
das Bett (-en)	bed	9			
das Bettlaken (-)	sheet	62	da	since	63
bezahlen	to pay	52	da	there	71
biegen	to bend	10	das Dach (¨er)	roof	58
die Biene (-n)	bee	9	danken	to thank	71
das Bild (-er)	picture	52	dann	then	71
billig	cheap	17	dauern	to last	41
der Bindfaden (¨)	string	68	der Daumen (-)	thumb	72
die Birne (-n)	pear	52	die Decke (-n)	blanket	10
bis	until	75	die Decke (-n)	ceiling	16
bitten	to ask	7	der Deckel (-)	lid	42
das Blatt (¨er)	leaf	41	denken	to think	71
blau	blue	11	der/die/das . . . da	that	71
bleiben	to stay	67	das Dia (-s)	slide	64
der Bleistift (-e)	pencil	52	der Diamant (-en)	diamond	23
blind	blind	10	dick	fat	28
der Blitz (-e)	lightning	43	dick	thick	71
blond	blond	11	dies	this	71
die Blume (-n)	flower	30	dieser/e/es	this	71
der Blumenkohl (-e)	cauliflower	16	das Ding (-e)	thing	71
die Blumenzwiebel (-n)	bulb	13	der Dinosaurier (-)	dinosaur	23
das Blut	blood	11	der Dirigent (-en)	conductor	20
der Boden (¨)	floor	29	das Dorf (¨er)	village	76
der Boden (¨)	ground	33	der Drachen (-)	dragon	24
die Bohne (-n)	bean	8	der Drachen (-)	kite	40
das Boot (-e)	boat	11	der Draht (¨e)	wire	79
braten	to fry	31	draußen	outside	50
die Bratpfanne (-n)	frying pan	31	das Dreieck (-e)	triangle	74
braun	brown	13	dumm	stupid	68
die Braut (¨e)	bride	12	dunkel	dark	22
der Bräutigam (-e)	bridegroom	12	dünn	thin	71
brechen	to break	12	durch	through	72
breit	wide	78	durstig	thirsty	71
brennen	to burn	13	duschen	to shower	63
der Brief (-e)	letter	42			
die Briefmarke (-n)	stamp	66	echt	real	57
die Brille (-n)	glasses	32	die Ecke (-n)	corner	20
bringen	to bring	12	das Ei (-er)	egg	26
das Brot	bread	12	der Eimer (-)	bucket	13
die Brücke (-n)	bridge	12	der Einbrecher (-)	burglar	13
der Bruder (¨)	brother	12	der Einbrecher (-)	thief	71
brüllen	to roar	58	einfrieren	to freeze	31
die Brust (¨e)	chest	17	der Eingang (¨e)	entrance	26
das Buch (¨er)	book	11	eingießen	to pour	55
die Bücherei (-n)	library	42	einige	some	65
die Buchhandlung (-en)	bookstore	11	einladen	to invite	38
buchstabieren	to spell	66	einwickeln	to wrap	80
das Bügeleisen (-)	iron	38	das Eis (-)	ice	37
bügeln	to iron	38	das Eis (-)	ice cream	37
der Bulle (-n)	bull	13	der Elefant (-en)	elephant	26
die Burg (-en)	castle	16	die Elfe (-n)	fairy	27
der Bürgersteig (-e)	sidewalk	63	der Ellbogen (-)	elbow	26
das Büro (-s)	office	49	die Eltern	parents	51
die Bürste (-n)	brush	13	das Ende (-n)	end	26
der Bus (-se)	bus	13	der Engel (-)	angel	5
der Busch (¨e)	bush	14	die Ente (-n)	duck	25
die Bushaltestelle (-n)	bus stop	14	entkommen	to escape	26
die Butter	butter	14	entlang	along	5
das Butterbrot (-e)	sandwich	60	die Erbse (-n)	pea	52
das Button (-s)	button	14	die Erdbeere (-n)	strawberry	68

German	English	Page	German	English	Page
die Erde	earth	25	die Frau (-en)	wife	78
erhalten	to receive	57	die Frau (-en)	woman	79
erkennen	to recognize	57	der Freund (-e)	(male) friend	31
erklären	to explain	27	die Freundin (-en)	(female) friend	31
erschrecken	to frighten	31	der Friseur (-e)	hairdresser	34
erster/e/es	first	29	der Frosch ("-e)	frog	31
erzählen	to tell	70	früh	early	25
der Esel (-)	donkey	24	das Frühstück (-e)	breakfast	12
essen	to eat	25	der Fuchs ("-e)	fox	30
das Essen	dinner	23	fühlen	to feel	28
das Essen	food	30	führen	to lead	41
das Eßzimmer (-)	dining room	23	füllen	to fill	29
etwas	something	65	der Füllfederhalter (-)	pen	52
die Eule (-n)	owl	50	für	for	30
das Experiment (-e)	experiment	27	der Fuß ("-e)	foot	28
			der Fußball	soccer	65
die Fabrik (-en)	factory	27	füttern	to feed	28
die Fahne (-n)	flag	29			
fahren	to drive	24	die Gabel (-n)	fork	30
die Fahrkarte (-n)	ticket	72	die Gans ("-e)	goose	33
das Fahrrad ("-er)	bicycle	10	das Garn (-e)	thread	71
fallen	to fall	27	der Garten (-)	garden	32
fallenlassen	to drop	24	das Gas	gas	32
der Fallschirm (-e)	parachute	51	der Gast ("-e)	guest	33
falsch	wrong	80	das Gebäude (-)	building	13
die Familie (-n)	family	27	geben	to give	32
fangen	to catch	16	der Geburtstag (-e)	birthday	10
die Farbe (-n)	color	19	die Gefahr (-en)	danger	22
die Farben	paints	50	gefrieren	to freeze	30
der Farbstift (-e)	crayon	20	das Gegenteil (-e)	opposite	49
fast	almost	5	gehen	to go	33
faul	lazy	41	gehören	to belong to	9
die Feder (-n)	feather	28	die Geige (-n)	violin	76
das Federbett (-en)	comforter	19	gelb	yellow	80
das Fell (-e)	fur	31	das Geld	money	46
der Felsen (-)	rock	58	das Gemüse (-)	vegetable	76
das Fenster (-)	window	79	genug	enough	26
das Fernsehen (-)	television	70	geöffnet	open	49
fertig	finished	29	der Gepäckträger (-)	bellboy	9
das Feuer (-)	bonfire	11	gerade	straight	68
das Feuer (-)	fire	29	das Geschäft (-e)	store	67
die Feuerwehrmänner	firemen	29	das Geschenk (-e)	present	55
das Feuerwerk (-e)	fireworks	29	die Geschichte (-n)	story	68
der Film (-e)	movie	46	das Gesicht (-er)	face	27
finden	to find	29	das Gespenst (-er)	ghost	32
der Finger (-)	finger	29	gestern	yesterday	80
der Fisch (-e)	fish	29	gestreift	striped	68
flach	flat	29	gewinnen	to win	79
die Flamme (-n)	flame	29	das Gewitter (-)	storm	67
die Flasche (-n)	bottle	11	die Giraffe (-n)	giraffe	32
der Fleck (-e)	spot	66	die Gitarre (-n)	guitar	34
das Fleisch	meat	45	das Glas ("-er)	glass	32
die Fliege (-n)	fly	30	das Glas ("-er)	jar	38
fliegen	to fly	30	glauben	to believe	9
fließen	to flow	30	gleich	same	60
der Flügel (-)	wing	79	die Glocke (-n)	bell	9
der Flughafen (-)	airport	5	glücklich	happy	35
das Flugzeug (-e)	airplane	5	das Gold	gold	33
der Fluß ("-sse)	river	58	graben	to dig	23
flüstern	to whisper	78	das Gras	grass	33
folgen	to follow	30	grau	gray	33
die Form (-en)	shape	62	der Griff (-e)	handle	34
das Foto (-s)	photograph	52	groß	big	10
der Fotoapparat (-e)	camera	15	groß	tall	70
die Frage (-n)	question	56	die Großstadt ("-e)	city	18

German	English	Page	German	English	Page
grün	green	33	das Huhn (¨er)	hen	36
die Gruppe (-n)	group	33	das Hühnchen (-)	chicken	17
die Gurke (-n)	cucumber	21	der Hund (-e)	dog	23
der Gürtel (-)	belt	9	das Hündchen (-)	puppy	55
gut	good	33	die Hundehütte (-n)	doghouse	24
			hungrig	hungry	37
das Haar (-e)	hair	34	hüpfen	to hop	36
die Haarbürste (-n)	hairbrush	34	husten	to cough	20
haben	to have	35	der Hut (¨e)	hat	35
der Hafen (¨)	harbor	35	die Hütte (-n)	shed	62
der Hafen (¨)	port	54			
der Hahn (¨e)	rooster	59	die Idee (-n)	idea	37
der Hai (-e)	shark	62	der Igel (-)	porcupine	54
der Haken (-)	hook	36	immer	always	5
halb	half	34	in	at	7
der Hals (¨e)	neck	47	in	in	38
halten	to hold	36	in . . . tun	to add	4
halten	to stop	67	das Insekt (-en)	insect	38
der Hamburger (-)	hamburger	34	die Insel (-n)	island	38
der Hammer (¨)	hammer	34			
die Hand (¨e)	hand	34	die Jacke (-n)	jacket	38
der Handschuh (-e)	glove	32	das Jahr (-e)	year	80
die Handtasche (-n)	handbag	34	die Jeans (-)	jeans	39
das Handtuch (¨er)	towel	73	jeder/e/es	any	6
hängen	to hang	34	jeder/e/es	each	25
hart	hard	35	jeder/e/es	every	26
häßlich	ugly	74	jemand	anybody	6
die Hauptstadt (¨e)	capital	15	jemand	someone	65
das Haus (¨er)	house	37	jetzt	now	48
die Hausaufgaben	homework	36	jung	young	80
die Haut	skin	64	der Junge (-n)	boy	12
die Hecke (-n)	hedge	35			
heiraten	to marry	45	der Kaffee	coffee	19
heiß	hot	37	der Käfig (-e)	cage	14
der Heizkörper (-)	radiator	37	das Kalb (¨er)	calf	15
helfen	to help	35	der Kalender (-)	calendar	15
hell	bright	12	kalt	cold	19
das Hemd (-en)	shirt	62	das Kamel (-e)	camel	15
herankommen	to reach	57	der Kamm (¨e)	comb	19
der Herd (-e)	stove	68	kämmen	to comb	19
das Herz (-en)	heart	35	das Känguruh (-s)	kangaroo	39
das Heu	hay	35	das Kaninchen (-)	rabbit	56
heute	today	72	die Kante (-n)	edge	26
die Hexe (-n)	witch	79	die Kapelle (-n)	band	8
hier	here	36	die Karotte (-n)	carrot	15
hierher	here	36	die Karte (-n)	cards	15
die Himbeere (-n)	raspberry	57	die Kartoffel (-n)	potato	55
der Himmel	sky	64	der Käse (-n)	cheese	17
hinauf	up	75	das Kätzchen (-)	kitten	40
hinter	behind	9	die Katze (-n)	cat	16
der Hirsch (-e)	deer	22	kaufen	to buy	14
hoch	high	36	der Keller (-)	cellar	16
hochheben	to lift	42	der Kellner (-)	waiter	76
die Hochzeit (-en)	wedding	77	kennen	to know (people)	40
höflich	polite	54	die Kerze (-n)	candle	15
die Höhle (-n)	cave	16	die Kette (-n)	chain	16
das Holz	wood	79	die Kette	necklace	47
der Honig	honey	36	das Kind (-er)	child	17
hören	to listen	43	der Kinderwagen (-)	baby carriage	7
hören	to hear	35	das Kinn (-e)	chin	17
die Hose (-n)	pants	51	das Kino (-s)	movie theater	47
das Hotel (-s)	hotel	37	die Kirche (-n)	church	18
hübsch	pretty	55	die Kirsche (-n)	cherry	17
der Hubschrauber (-)	helicopter	35	das Kissen (-)	cushion	21
der Hügel (-)	hill	36	die Klasse (-n)	class	18

das Klassenzimmer (-)	classroom	18
das Klavier (-e)	piano	52
das Kleid (-er)	dress	24
klein	small	64
der Kleinbus	van	75
klettern	to climb	18
klingeln	to ring	58
die Klippe (-n)	cliff	18
klopfen	to knock	40
klug	clever	18
kneifen	to pinch	53
das Knie (-)	knee	40
der Knochen (-)	bone	11
die Knospe (-n)	bud	13
der Knoten (-)	knot	40
knüpfen	to tie	72
kochen	to cook	20
der Koffer (-)	suitcase	69
der Kohlkopf (¨e)	cabbage	14
kommen	to come	19
der König (-e)	king	39
die Königin (-en)	queen	56
können	to know how to	40
der Kopf (¨e)	head	35
das Kopfkissen (-)	pillow	53
der Korb (¨e)	basket	8
der Korken (-)	cork	20
der Körper (-)	body	11
kosten	to cost	20
das Kotelett (-e)	chop	17
der Krake (-n)	octopus	49
der Kran (-e)	crane	20
krank	ill	38
das Krankenhaus (¨er)	hospital	37
die Krankenschwester (-)	nurse	49
der Krankenwagen (-)	ambulance	5
kratzen	to scratch	61
die Krawatte (-n)	tie	72
der Krebs (-e)	crab	20
die Kreide	chalk	16
der Kreis (-e)	circle	18
das Kreuz (-e)	cross	21
die Kreuzung (-en)	intersection	38
der Krieg (-e)	war	77
das Krokodil (-e)	crocodile	21
die Krone (-n)	crown	21
der Krug (¨e)	pitcher	53
die Küche (-n)	kitchen	40
der Kuchen (-)	cake	14
der Küchenschrank (¨e)	cupboard	21
die Kuh (¨e)	cow	20
der Kühlschrank (¨e)	refrigerator	57
das Küken (-)	chick	17
der Kunde (-n)	customer	21
der Künstler (-)	artist	7
kurz	short	62
küssen	to kiss	40
die Küste (-n)	coast	19
lächeln	to smile	64
lachen	to laugh	41
das Lamm (¨er)	lamb	41
die Lampe (-n)	lamp	41
das Land (¨er)	country	20
die Landkarte (-n)	map	44
lang	long	43
langsam	slowly	64
der Lärm (-)	noise	48
der Lastwagen (-)	truck	74
laufen	to run	59
laut	loud	44
das Leben	life	42
leben	to live	43
der Lebensmittel-händler (-)	grocer	33
lecken	to lick	42
das Leder	leather	42
leer	empty	26
leeren	to empty	26
der Lehrer (-)	teacher	70
leicht	easy	25
leicht	light	42
die Leine (-n)	leash	41
leise	quiet	56
die Leiter (-n)	ladder	40
lernen	to learn	41
lesen	to read	57
letzter/e/es	last	41
der Leuchtturm (¨e)	lighthouse	43
die Leute	people	52
das Licht (-er)	light	42
lieben	to love	44
das Lied (-er)	song	65
der Lift (-s)	elevator	26
lila	purple	55
links	left	42
die Lippe (-n)	lip	43
die Liste (-n)	list	43
das Loch (¨er)	hole	36
der Löffel (-)	spoon	66
die Lösung (-en)	answer	6
der Löwe (-n)	lion	43
die Luft	air	4
lustig	funny	31
machen	to make	44
das Mädchen (-)	girl	32
malen	to paint	50
manchmal	sometimes	65
der Mann (¨er)	husband	37
der Mann (¨er)	man	44
die Mannschaft (-en)	team	70
der Mantel (¨)	coat	19
die Marionette (-n)	puppet	55
der Markt (¨e)	market	44
die Marmelade	jam	38
die Maschine (-n)	machine	44
die Maske (-n)	mask	45
der Matrose (-n)	sailor	60
die Mauer (-n)	wall	76
die Maus (¨e)	mouse	46
die Medizin (-en)	medicine	45
das Meer (-e)	sea	61
das Mehl	flour	30
mehr	more	46
die meisten	most	46
eine Menge	a lot of	43
messen	measure	45
das Messer (-)	knife	40
das Metall (-e)	metal	45

der Metzger (-)	butcher	14
die Milch	milk	45
die Minute (-n)	minute	45
mit	with	79
das Mittagessen (-)	lunch	44
die Mitte	middle	45
das Modell (-e)	model	46
mögen	to like	43
der Monat (-e)	month	46
der Mond (-e)	moon	46
der Morgen (-)	morning	46
morgen	tomorrow	73
morgens	in the morning	46
das Motorrad (-̈er)	motorcycle	46
müde	tired	72
die Mülltonne (-n)	garbage can	32
der Mund (-̈er)	mouth	47
die Münze (-n)	coin	19
die Muschel (-n)	shell	62
die Musik	music	47
die Mutter (-̈)	mother	46
nach	after	4
nachmittag	afternoon	4
die Nacht (-̈e)	night	48
die Nadel (-n)	needle	48
der Nagel (-̈)	nail	47
nahe	near	47
nähen	to sew	61
die Nähmaschine (-n)	sewing machine	61
der Name (-n)	name	47
die Nase (-n)	nose	48
naß	wet	77
der Nebel	fog	30
neben	next to	48
nehmen	to take	70
das Nest (-er)	nest	48
nett	kind	39
neu	new	48
nichts	nothing	48
nie	never	48
niedrig	low	44
niemand	nobody	48
das Nilpferd (-e)	hippopotamus	36
noch ein	another	6
der Norden	north	48
nötig haben	to need	47
das Notizbuch (-̈er)	notebook	48
nur	only	49
die Nuß (-̈sse)	nut	49
nützlich	useful	75
ob	if	38
oben	top	73
oben	upstairs	75
das Obst	fruit	31
der Obstkuchen (-)	pie	53
oder	or	50
öffnen	to open	49
oft	often	49
ohne	without	79
das Ohr (-en)	ear	25
ölen	to oil	49
der Onkel (-)	uncle	75

orangefarbig	orange	50
ordnen	to arrange	6
der Ort (-e)	place	53
der Osten	east	25
das Ostern (-)	Easter	25
das Paar (-e)	pair	50
das Paket (-e)	package	50
der Palast (-̈e)	palace	51
die Pampelmuse (-n)	grapefruit	33
der Pantoffel (-n)	slipper	64
der Papagei (-en)	parrot	51
das Papier (-e)	paper	51
der Park (-s)	park	51
parken	to park	51
die Party (-s)	party	51
der Paß (-̈sse)	passport	51
passieren	to happen	35
der Patient (-en)	patient	51
der Pfannkuchen (-)	pancake	51
der Pfeffer	pepper	52
die Pfeife (-n)	pipe	53
der Pfeil (-e)	arrow	6
das Pferd (-e)	horse	36
der Pfirsich (-e)	peach	52
die Pflanze (-n)	plant	53
pflanzen	to plant	53
pflücken	to pick	52
die Pfote (-n)	paw	51
das Picknick (-e)	picnic	52
der Pilot (-en)	pilot	53
der Pilz (-e)	mushroom	47
die Pistole (-n)	gun	34
die Planierraupe (-n)	bulldozer	13
der Platz (-̈e)	place	53
plötzlich	suddenly	68
polieren	to polish	54
der Polizist (-en)	policeman	54
die Pommes frites	French fries	31
das Pony (-s)	pony	54
das Portemonnaie (-s)	purse	55
die Post	post office	54
der Postbote (-n)	mailman	44
die Postkarte (-n)	postcard	54
der Preis (-e)	price	55
der Preis (-e)	prize	55
probieren	to taste	70
der Pudding (-e)	pudding	55
die Puppe (-n)	doll	24
das Puzzle (-s)	puzzle	56
das Quadrat (-e)	square	66
quer über	across	4
das Rad (-̈er)	wheel	78
das Radio (-s)	radio	56
der Rasen (-)	lawn	41
der Rasierapparat (-e)	razor	57
die Ratte (-n)	rat	57
rauchen	to smoke	64
der Rauhreif	frost	31
die Raupe (-n)	caterpillar	16
recht	right	58
der Regenbogen (-)	rainbow	57
der Regenmantel (-̈)	raincoat	57

der Regenschirm (-e)	umbrella	74
regnen	to rain	57
reiben	to rub	59
reich	rich	58
der Reifen (-)	tire	72
die Reihe (-n)	row	59
der Reis	rice	58
reiten	to ride	58
rennen	to race	56
reparieren	to fix	29
die Richtung (-en)	direction	23
riechen	to smell	64
der Riese (-n)	giant	32
das Rindfleisch	beef	9
der Ring (-e)	ring	58
der Rock (¨e)	skirt	64
rosa	pink	53
die Rose (-n)	rose	59
rot	red	57
der Rücken (-)	back	7
rudern	to row	59
rufen	to call	15
rund	round	59
rutschen	to slide	64
der Sack (¨e)	sack	59
die Säge (-n)	saw	60
sagen	to say	60
die Sahne	cream	21
der Salat (-e)	lettuce	42
der Salat (-e)	salad	60
das Salz	salt	60
der Same (-n)	seed	61
der Sand	sand	60
die Sandale (-n)	sandal	60
der Satz (¨e)	sentence	61
sauber	clean	18
sauber machen	to clean	18
die Schachtel (-n)	box	12
das Schaf (-e)	sheep	62
der Schal (-s)	scarf	60
die Schale (-n)	bowl	11
die Schallplatte (-n)	record	57
scharf	sharp	62
der Schatten (-)	shadow	61
der Schatz (¨e)	treasure	74
die Schaufel (-n)	shovel	63
die Schaukel (-n)	swing	69
der Schauspieler (-)	actor	4
der Scheck (-s)	check	17
die Scheibe (-n)	slice	64
scheinen	to seem	61
der Scheinwerfer (-)	headlight	35
schenken	to offer	49
die Schere (-n)	scissors	61
der Schi (-er)	ski	63
Schi laufen	to ski	64
schicken	to send	43
das Schiff (-e)	ship	62
der Schimpanse (-n)	chimpanzee	17
der Schinken	ham	34
der Schlafanzug (¨e)	pyjamas	56
schlafen	to sleep	64
das Schlafzimmer (-)	bedroom	9
schlagen	to hit	36

die Schlägermütze (-n)	cap	15
der Schlamm	mud	47
die Schlange (-n)	snake	65
schlecht	bad	7
die Schleife (-n)	ribbon	58
schließen	to close	18
schlimm	bad	7
Schlittschuh laufen	to skate	63
schlucken	to swallow	69
der Schlüssel (-)	key	39
schmelzen	to melt	45
der Schmetterling (-e)	butterfly	14
der Schmuck	jewels	39
schmutzig	dirty	23
der Schnabel (¨)	beak	8
die Schnecke (-n)	snail	65
schneiden	to cut	21
schneien	to snow	65
schnell	fast	28
schnell laufen	to hurry	37
der Schnurrbart (¨e)	mustache	47
die Schokolade	chocolate	17
schon	already	5
schön	beautiful	9
der Schornstein (-e)	chimney	17
der Schrank (¨e)	closet	18
schreiben	to write	80
die Schreibmaschine (-n)	typewriter	74
Schreibmaschine schreiben	to type	74
der Schreibtisch (-e)	desk	23
schreien	to yell	80
der Schubkarren (-)	wheelbarrow	78
der Schuh (-e)	shoe	62
die Schule (-n)	school	61
der Schulranzen (-)	knapsack	40
die Schulter (-n)	shoulder	62
die Schürze (-n)	apron	6
die Schüssel (-n)	dish	23
schütteln	to shake	62
schwach	weak	77
der Schwan (¨e)	swan	69
der Schwanz (¨e)	tail	69
schwarz	black	10
das Schwein (-e)	pig	53
das Schweinefleisch	pork	54
schwer	heavy	35
die Schwester (-n)	sister	63
das Schwimmbad (¨er)	swimming pool	69
schwimmen	to swim	69
der See (-n)	lake	41
der Seehund (-e)	seal	61
das Segelboot (-e)	sailboat	60
segeln	to sail	59
sehen	to see	61
sehr	very	76
die Seife (-n)	soap	65
die Seifenblase (-n)	bubble	13
das Seil (-e)	rope	59
seit	since	63
die Seite (-n)	page	50
die Seite (-n)	side	63
der Sessel (-)	easy chair	25
die Shorts	shorts	62
sich ansehen	to look at	43

sich ausruhen	to rest	58	die Strickjacke (-n)	sweater	69
sich aussuchen	to choose	17	der Strumpf ("e)	stocking	67
sich entschließen	to decide	22	die Strumpfhose (-n)	tights	72
sich erinnern	to remember	58	das Stück (-e)	piece	53
sich lehnen	to lean	41	die Stufen	stairs	66
sich schlagen	to fight	28	der Stuhl ("e)	chair	16
sich streiten	to argue	6	die Stunde (-n)	hour	37
sich trauen	to dare	22	suchen	to look for	43
sich verfahren	to get lost	43	der Süden	south	66
sich verstecken	hide	36	der Supermarkt ("e)	supermarket	69
sich weigern	to refuse	57	die Suppe (-n)	soup	66
sicher	safe	59	die Süßigkeit (-en)	candy	15
silbern	silver	63			
singen	to sing	63	die Tafel (-n)	blackboard	10
sitzen	to sit	63	der Tag (-e)	day	22
so tun, als ob	to pretend	55	das Tal ("er)	valley	75
so . . . wie	as	7	die Tante (-n)	aunt	7
die Socke (-n)	sock	65	tanzen	to dance	22
das Sofa (-s)	sofa	65	die Tänzerin (-en)	dancer	22
der Sohn ("e)	son	65	die Tapete	wallpaper	76
der Soldat (-en)	soldier	65	die Tasche (-n)	bag	7
die Sonne	sun	69	die Tasche (-n)	pocket	54
die Sorte (-n)	kind	39	der Taschenrechner (-)	calculator	15
die Soße (-n)	sauce	60	das Taschentuch ("er)	handkerchief	34
spät	late	41	die Tasse (-n)	cup	21
der Spaziergang ("e)	walk	76	das Taxi (-s)	taxi	70
die Speisekarte (-n)	menu	45	der Teddybär (-en)	teddy bear	70
der Spiegel (-)	mirror	45	der Tee	tea	70
das Spiel (-e)	game	31	die Teekanne (-n)	teapot	70
spielen	to play	54	der Teich (-e)	pond	54
das Spielzeug (-e)	toy	73	teilen	to share	62
die Spinne (-n)	spider	66	das Telefon (-e)	telephone	70
das Spinnengewebe (-)	cobweb	19	der Teller (-)	plate	54
die Spitze	lace	40	das Tennis	tennis	71
sprechen	to speak	66	der Teppich (-e)	carpet	15
springen	to jump	39	das Theater (-)	theater	71
die Stadt ("e)	town	73	tief	deep	22
der Stall ("e)	stable	66	das Tier (-e)	animal	6
der Stapel (-)	pile	53	der Tiger (-)	tiger	72
stark	strong	68	der Tisch (-e)	table	69
die Statue (-n)	statue	67	die Tochter (")	daughter	22
der Staub	dust	25	die Tomate (-n)	tomato	72
der Staubsauger (-)	vacuum cleaner	75	der Topf ("e)	pot	55
die Stecknadel (-n)	pin	53	das Tor (-e)	gate	32
stehen	to stand	66	tot	dead	22
stehlen	to steal	67	töten	to kill	39
der Stein (-e)	stone	67	tragen	to carry	16
stellen	to put	56	tragen	to wear	77
der Stengel (-)	stem	67	der Traktor (-en)	tractor	73
sterben	to die	23	die Träne (-n)	tear	70
die Stereoanlage (-n)	stereo	67	träumen	to dream	24
der Stern (-e)	star	67	traurig	sad	59
der Stiefel (-)	boot	11	treffen	to meet	45
die Stimme (-n)	voice	76	die Treppe	stairs	66
die Stirn (-en)	forehead	30	treten	to kick	39
der Stock ("e)	stick	67	die Trillerpfeife (-n)	whistle	78
stoßen	to push	56	trinken	to drink	24
der Strand ("e)	beach	8	trocken	dry	25
die Straße (-n)	road	58	die Trommel (-n)	drum	25
die Straße (-n)	street	68	die Trompete (-n)	trumpet	74
der Strauß ("e)	bunch	13	tropfen	to leak	41
streichen	to spread	66	die Tulpe (-n)	tulip	74
das Streichholz ("er)	match	45	tun	to do	23
die Strickarbeit (-en)	knitting	40	die Tür (-en)	door	24
stricken	to knit	40	der Turm ("e)	tower	73

die U-Bahn	subway	68
über	above	4
über	over	50
überall	everywhere	27
überqueren	to cross	21
die Überraschung (-en)	surprise	69
das Übungsheft (-e)	workbook	80
das Ufer (-)	bank	8
die Uhr (-en)	clock	18
die Uhr (-en)	watch	77
um	at	7
um ... herum stehen	to surround	69
der Umschlag (¨e)	envelope	26
umstellen	to move	46
und	and	5
uneben	rough	59
die Unebenheit (-en)	bump	13
der Unfall (¨e)	accident	4
das Ungeheuer (-)	monster	46
ungezogen	naughty	47
unglücklich	unhappy	75
unten	bottom	11
unten	downstairs	24
unter	below	9
unter	under	75
die Unterrichtsstunde (-n)	lesson	42
das Unterseeboot (-e)	submarine	68
die Untertasse (-n)	saucer	60
der Urlaub (-e)	vacation	75
die Vase (-n)	vase	76
der Vater (¨)	father	28
verbinden	to join	39
verfolgen	to chase	16
vergessen	to forget	30
verkaufen	to sell	61
verlassen	to leave	42
verletzen	to hurt	37
verpassen	to miss	45
verschieden	different	23
versprechen	to promise	55
verstehen	to understand	75
viel	much	47
viele	many	44
vielleicht	perhaps	52
der Vogel (¨)	bird	10
voll	full of	31
von	about	4
von	from	31
vor	before	9
vor	in front of	31
vorbeigehen	to pass by	51
der Vorhang (¨e)	curtain	21
vorher	before	9
die Waage (-n)	scale	60
wachsen	to grow	33
der Wagen (-)	car	15
während	while	78
der Wald (¨er)	forest	30
die Wange (-n)	cheek	16
wann	when	78
warm	warm	77
die Warnung (-en)	sign	63

warten	to wait	76
warum	why	78
was	what	78
das Waschbecken (-)	sink	63
waschen	to wash	77
die Waschmaschine (-n)	washing machine	77
das Wasser	water	77
der Wasserfall (¨e)	waterfall	77
der Wasserhahn (¨e)	faucet	28
der Wasserkessel (-)	kettle	39
das Wechselgeld	change	16
wechseln	to change	16
der Wecker (-)	alarm clock	5
der Weg (-e)	path	51
wegblasen	(to blow) away	7
weich	soft	65
die Weide (-n)	field	28
Weihnachten	Christmas	18
weil	because	9
weinen	to cry	21
die Weintraube (-n)	grape	33
weiß	white	78
weit	far	28
der Weizen	wheat	78
welcher/e/es	which	78
die Welle (-n)	wave	77
die Welt	world	80
der Weltraum	space	66
wenig	few	28
wenn	if	38
wenn	when	78
wer	who	78
werfen	to throw	72
die Werkstatt (¨en)	garage	32
das Werkzeug (-e)	tool	73
die Wespe (-n)	wasp	77
der Westen	west	78
wichtig	important	38
wie	how	37
wieder	again	4
der Wind (-e)	wind	79
die Windmühle (-n)	windmill	79
wissen	to know (things)	40
der Witz (-e)	joke	39
wo	where	78
die Wohnung (-en)	apartment	6
der Wohnwagen (-)	trailer	74
das Wohnzimmer (-)	living room	43
die Wolke (-n)	cloud	19
die Wolle	wool	79
wollen	to want	76
das Wort (¨er)	word	79
das Wörterbuch (¨er)	dictionary	23
der Würfel (-)	cube	21
der Wurm (¨er)	worm	80
das Würstchen (-)	sausage	60
das Würstchen (-)	hot dog	37
die Wurzel (-n)	root	59
die Wüste (-n)	desert	22
wütend	angry	6
die Zahl (-en)	number	48
zählen	to count	20
der Zahnarzt (¨e)	dentist	22
die Zahnbürste (-n)	toothbrush	73

German	English	Page	German	English	Page
die Zähne	teeth	70	ziehen	to pull	55
die Zahnpasta	toothpaste	73	ziemlich	quite	56
der Zauberer (-)	magician	44	das Zimmer (-)	room	58
der Zaun (¨e)	fence	28	der Zirkus (-se)	circus	18
das Zebra (-s)	zebra	80	die Zitrone (-n)	lemon	42
die Zehe (-n)	toe	72	der Zoo (-s)	zoo	80
das Zeichen (-)	mark	44	zu	at	7
zeichnen	to draw	24	zu	shut	63
die Zeichnung (-en)	drawing	24	zu	to	72
zeigen	to point	54	zu	too	73
zeigen	to show	63	der Zucker	sugar	68
die Zeitschrift (-en)	magazine	44	der Zug (¨e)	train	74
die Zeitung (-en)	newspaper	48	die Zunge (-n)	tongue	73
das Zelt (-e)	tent	71	zusammen	together	72
!ten	to camp	15	die Zwiebel (-n)	onion	49
rreißen	to tear	70	der Zwilling (-e)	twin	74
ə Ziege (-n)	goat	33	zwischen	among	5
ər Ziegelstein (-e)	brick	12	zwischen	between	10